CUBA
<u>**Escape From Paradise**</u>
By Joey Infante

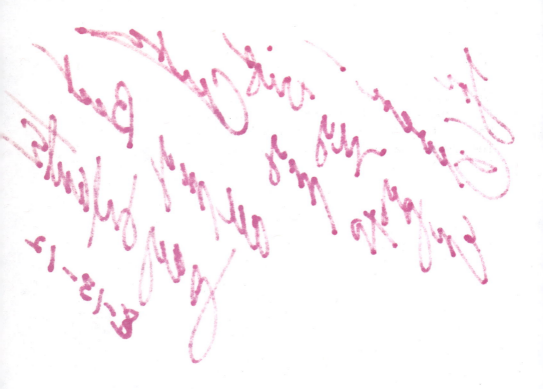

© 2005 Joseph Infante

All rights reserved. Except for brief passages quoted in a newspaper, magazine, radio, television or internet review, no part of this book may be reproduced or transmitted in any form, or by any means, electronic or mechanical, including photocopying or recording, or by any information storage and retrieval system, without permission in writing from the author and publisher.

ISBN 0-9676719-2-2

Library of Congress Control Number: 2004195071

Book/Cover Design, and Layout by Soraida Martinez
Published 1/28/05

Cover Painting: Le Coq D'Or © 2002 Joseph Infante
Cover Photograph by Rik Davis

Artist, Soraida
PO BOX 32
Gibbsboro, New Jersey 08026
soraida@soraida.com

CONTENTS

Dedication/Acknowledgments...1
The Famous Canastilla Award...2
The Old Flamboyán Tree...2
The Crazy Chicken...3
The Old Hag...3
The Goat..4
Papá...5
Kary's House...5
The White Stallion..5
The Old School House..6
Deanna Durbin..7
The Courting Square...7
Bobby Capó and Bobby Collazo...8
El Centro Gallego...8
The Stroke of Life..9
THE STORY: From JFK to Cancún, Destination Havana.....................9
HAVANA: At José Martí International Airport............................14
The Tour..19
The Tropicana Nightclub...22
Havana Café...25
The Next Day...26
Regla..27
The Santero's Store...31
Getting Back to Havana..32
La Capital...33
The H. Upmann Tobacco Factory...33
Chinatown..34
An Art Exhibition..35
El Malecón...36
The Stalker..37
The Visit..37
Learning To Drive..39
Back to The Visit..40
At Dracula's Castle (The Hospital)....................................42

Coppelia's...46
The Prostitute...46
Peeping Into Windows..47
In America...48
Back to Window Peeping...49
El Morro Castle...51
The Escape...56
Varadero Beach..59
Entering Paradise...63
Hotel Sol Palmeras...66
My Feathered Friend...67
At The Beach..70
David..72
Shark Attack...73
A Clawless Lobster...77
The Lovers..80
Santiago...86
El Cobre...93
The Market..95
A Case of Intestinal Flu...96
Back to The Market...97
Guardalavaca Beach in Banes....................................102
Banes...107
Poem: Cuba..119
Joey's Family Tree..120
Photographs and Paintings..121

El Morro Castle (The Lighthouse)

DEDICATION

This book is dedicated to my parents, María Luz Castellanos and Sandalio Infante, who worked so hard to escape from their Cuban paradise—even when, at the time, there wasn't a need to do so. Under the regime of Fulgencio Batista, one had to abandon the homeland and travel elsewhere, if one wanted a better life; the great USA was the chosen land. So, with five children in tow, my parents headed for this promise land—where, as some say, "the streets are paved with gold." Better housing and education were foremost on the list of wants. We never did find the streets of gold, but we did find a land filled with many opportunities.

ACKNOWLEDGMENTS

I want to thank my close friends, for all the positive input and advice that I have received throughout the creation of this book—especially, James M. McDonald, for being there for me every step of the way, making sure "I did it my way." Also on the list are my editors, in order of progress, James M. McDonald, Lorna Doran, Victor Edgar Rivera, and my publisher, Soraida Martinez—for their dedication to this project. Much gratitude goes to my family, for their stories, names, and addresses, all of which helped me find my way back home. I offer this journey to my compatriots, who were also, at an early age, taken to a different world, and are unable to return to the "Motherland"—all because of one man's political quest for domination—one man's omission of the heartfelt feelings of mothers, daughters, fathers, sons, and families—whom they will never see again, until they meet in the endless boundaries of Heaven. So for you, "Comrades,"—as well as for myself—I have made this illicit journey in search of my Cuban Roots. Through my eyes, my words and photographs, you too will find a piece of your own beginnings. Be patient, dear friends, we shall soon be free!

The Famous Canastilla Award

On a hot, sultry night on January 28, 1941, the screams of a lady giving birth were heard throughout the neighborhood; the person responsible for causing this pain was me. I was born in the small town of *Banes*, *Oriente*, Cuba—at exactly the same date and hour as our Cuban hero and patriot, *José Martí,* a poet and ideologist who fought to his death in the first Cuban revolution against the Spanish. This made me the recipient of the famous *Canastilla* award.

The prize consisted of several women throughout the island spending many hours embroidering baby clothes, diapers, formal suits, hats, socks, blankets; everything that a baby would need in his first two years on earth—which also included a crib and a stroller. (A King's ransom was granted to the kid from a middle class family.) We had all the necessities—such as food, clothing, and a roof over our heads. There was money for recreation, but we were far from ready to move into the 6-white-column, 4-bedroom-house on the hill.

The Old Flamboyán Tree

I was the fifth child to be conceived; and, as the story goes, I was not planned. Papá was off to work the sugar cane harvest but, before he departed, there was something that he wanted—because he would not see Mamá for several months. Mamá was left with a package; and when Papá returned, he had seven pounds of happiness to bounce on his knees.

I close my eyes and I can clearly remember my childhood homes: one of them had a tree growing in the center of the kitchen. The thick trunk made its way out through the ceiling, while its branches rested on the roof; that's where I was born. Papá didn't have the heart to cut down the beautiful tree, so he built the house around it. Although the ceiling was sealed around the tree, on rainy days enough water would seep down the trunk and water its roots. The floor was cut in a circle, a foot away from the tree, with chicken wire placed around its base to keep unwanted little critters from entering the house. Papá loved the old *flamboyán* tree; from a distance, during a bright sunset, the red *flamboyán* flowers on the roof made our home look like it was on fire.

The Crazy Chicken

I was a very mischievous child. Mamá had a gray and white chicken tied to an iron bar that rested on top of a small wooden table and I would poke that bird with a stick—just to see it fly up in the air and make loud clucking sounds. Of course, the commotion would agitate my sister's dog, and it would bark hysterically and upset the whole household. Everyone would rush to the kitchen, thinking that something awful had happened to me; instead, they would find a chicken doing somersaults, a dog barking at the crazed flying bird, and me sitting on the floor—laughing uncontrollably. There would be so much noise and excitement: my sister yelling at the dog to quiet it down, Mamá trying to calm the brainless chicken, which was flying all over the place—refusing to get caught. Meanwhile the iron bar tied to the hen's leg fell off the table and came crashing down on my hand—cutting my thumb. The noise stopped when my cries of pain were heard above the hysteria and blood was splattered all over my hands and face. Mamá came quickly to my aid and almost went crazy when she saw that a piece of my thumb was missing—that's when she rushed me to the clinic and they gave me five stitches.

Nowadays, I have a half-inch scar across the tip of my thumb; every time I look at it, I remember the chicken.

The Old Hag

The second house that I lived in had bars on the windows—from which I used to hang and drive Mamá crazy. There was a deep well in the back yard into which I once threw an angry cat and Papá had to scale down the well walls and send the cat back up in a bucket. He wasn't very happy about that; I had put his life in danger in order to save that mean, wet, old cat that belonged to the old and nasty hag that lived down the road.

The old nag was just as mean as her cat—and just as ugly; every time she passed my house, she would attract my attention and stick her tongue out at me. I told Mamá several times what she did and Mamá would tell me to just ignore the crazy woman. The old hag stuck her tongue out at me a couple of more times and, on the third time, I had enough—so I threw a rock that smacked her in the middle of her head. One never heard such screaming! A short while later, the witch's son, carrying a machete, came looking for Papá. He held Papá responsible for my indiscretion, but Papá feared no one! Papá took to his machete to defend himself and there they were, two grown men going around in circles, yelling at each other—while the women screamed—trying to break up the fight. I was scared and crying, hanging on to Mamá's skirt, while she yelled at Papá to stop the fighting. It didn't get too crazy and no one got hurt, but "macho-men" have to defend their honor. The whole neighborhood knew what happened and every time they'd see me, they'd shake a finger at me. (Boy, I wish I knew sign language back then!)

The Goat

Soon, all returned to normal and I continued climbing trees and acquiring a stomachache from eating too many mangos and bananas. I was raised drinking goat's milk, instead of cow's milk; so after Juana's death (that was the goat's name), Papá bought me my own goat—she was gorgeous. My goat was black and white, with big brown eyes and long, black, luxurious lashes. Mamá would milk her every day, then boil the milk to sterilize it before serving. I would skim the fat off the top of the boiled milk, add sugar, and eat it for desert; that was a real treat.

One morning Mamá caught me standing on top of a pail, trying to seduce the goat. How embarrassing! Mamá screamed and I ran for my life. I didn't have to pull my pants up—I was already bottomless from playing in the back yard. This gave me a head start in running, but Mamá caught me and gave me the beating of my life. Mamá had never spanked me this rough before, so I guess I must have done something very wrong. After a severe scolding, Mamá made me apologize to the goat.

From Mamá, I learned to respect and love all animals, and never to abuse or harm them. I was just following my instincts, but they were the wrong ones. I never tried to seduce the goat again, but it did cross my mind once or twice.

Papá

Papá was a family man: strong, brave, "macho," sensitive, and—most of all—a loving father. Papá would take me to an open field and pitch baseballs to me. Once in a great while, I would hit a ball, but I spent most of the time retrieving them. You see, I was standing downhill—I was never good at the manly art of baseball. But Papá never lost his patience with me. Papá would sit me on his shoulders for hours—so that I could watch a parade. At the beach, I would stand on his strong hands and use them as a trampoline to dive into the water. They all called me, "shark," because I swam so well. Our playing was rough, but it always ended with a big hug and lots of laughter.

Kary's House

The third, and last house, we lived in—before coming to America—was owned by my sister, Kary, and her family. It was a two-family wooden house, with a big front porch, and a lovely back yard. We lived on the ground level, which had a dirt floor. Mamá would sprinkle water on the earth in order to sweep it, and to keep the dirt from flying into the air. In 1946 we didn't have modern conveniences; I don't remember how Mamá cooked our food, but we ate well.

There was an iron frame bed, with squeaky steel springs, that Mamá and I shared. We tried not to move too much, because the squeaks would awaken each other's sleep. Each side of the bed was hollowed out from too much use and it felt as if we were sleeping in a hole. Sometimes, we would get pinched by a broken spring or—if we rolled over far enough—we would land in the other's hollow side. My sisters, Melba and Misael, had their own similar bedroom.

The White Stallion

The man in the house next to us owned a beautiful white stallion and, every once in a while, he would sit me on the horse and give me a ride. One day, we were all awakened by men shouting and giving orders. It seems that the horse was grazing during the night, got too close to the cistern buried in the backyard of my sister's house, and fell through the soft earth. The men tried to get the stubborn horse out by pulling on the ropes tied to its neck. The stallion struggled to get out but—instead—dug itself deeper into the hole. Instincts must have told the stallion to sit still, because it stayed quiet for some time; suddenly, with great effort to escape, the horse gave with all of its might one last leap for survival—as the men pulled on the tight ropes that could have strangled the great animal. The horse finally rose out of the cistern and collapsed from exhaustion.

Afterwards, the men washed the animal and returned him to its white glory. The regal stallion continued grazing—as if nothing had happened. The cistern was filled with cement and it was safe again. We lived at Kary's for one year. Papá and my brother, Rodolfo, were already in America—paving the way for the rest of the family.

The Old School House

I was growing up fast and, at the age of five, I went to kindergarten. We didn't have a formal school in *Banes*; there was only an old house at the top of a hill, with a teacher and a few schoolroom-type chairs. We learned to draw circles and lines representing raindrops, and played games like hide-n-seek.

My favorite place to hide was in the garden, where the flowers were huge and colorful, about five times the size of my small hands. I would wrap myself with the giant yellow-green leaves of the banana tree and hide from my friends; here, I could hear the flapping wings of the butterflies, as they flew past me, exhibiting their intricate designs and iridescent colors. The butterflies must have been at least twelve inches long—or—I thought they were.

Sometimes, the palm trees, silhouetted on a red-orange sunset, scared the life out of me; they reminded me of giant, hairy, tarantula spiders waving in the gentle breeze.

Now, whenever I see a palm tree, I'm taken back to the time when I saw the world through the eyes of an enchanted child—the world seemed a bit scary then.

6

Deanna Durbin

There was a playground that I enjoyed, which had swings and monkey bars and dizzying rides that went round and round. There was also a movie theater, where I saw my first movie and fell in love with Deanna Durbin. Later on—as an adult—I discovered the name of this movie that started my great love affair with Deanna; it was called, "I Could Go On Singing." One scene that I will never forget was when the cowboy was lying down by the edge of a riverbank drinking water; Deanna approached him quietly from behind, lifted her long dress up and—with her foot—dunked his head in the water. That was something I would do; so, from then on, Deanna and I were pals.

It was rumored that Deanna had a glass eye and that this was the reason her eyes sparkled so much on screen. Some say it was her arms—one shorter than the other—that were her handicap. I loved her even more for not being perfect. To this day, I'm not really certain if Deanna did or did not have a glass eye. I don't care—I love her anyway.

The Courting Square

In front of the theater, there was a large park or square, where people would gather in the evening and stroll counter-clockwise and socialize with friends. The women usually walked in groups: if a woman faced the outside of the park, this meant that she was available or looking for a boyfriend; walking on the inside of the park meant that she was spoken for or married—hands off! Usually, the married women received most of the attention. Maybe it was that "lived in" look, or the rounded figure, or just that secure, "I'm not looking" look, that compelled men to pursue the married ladies.

The park had huge, round cement planters, where *flamboyán* trees and colorful flowers grew; benches were placed around the planters for sitting and courting; turn-of-the-century wrought-iron street lanterns lined the perimeter of the park. In my memories, it all looked so beautiful. Of course, at the time, I was still a young terror—weaving in and out between people—as hard knuckles landed on my head for getting in the way or for pinching someone's butt. Some of those knuckles really did hurt, so I didn't get away pain-free.

Bobby Capó and Bobby Collazo

The best part of the evening was going to my favorite ice cream parlor, which was located on the balcony of the Hernandez Theater. There I would sit near the jukebox and play my favorite song over and over again: *"La última noche que pasé contigo"* (The Last Night That We Spent Together)—which was sung by Bobby Capó, a Puerto Rican singer whom I had the pleasure of meeting later in my theatrical years. I also befriended and worked with Bobby Collazo, the Cuban composer of the song. Collazo wrote a special musical arrangement of this song for me to introduce during my cabaret years. Bobby and Bobby were both flattered when they found out that their adult song had appealed to a boy of 5 years old. I have always been older than my years—now, I'm just trying to stay young.

El Centro Gallego

The houses that lined the park were beautiful and I remember one in particular. It was a large, white, art-deco mansion—with pillars, arched doorways, and huge rooms with shiny marble floors. The mansion was called, *El Centro Gallego* (The Spanish Club). It was for members only and my father proudly belonged to it. We attended a costume party there—the memory of which still plays in my mind from time to time. There were many people in lavish costumes and masks—dancing to the rhythm of the *Danzón*, a slow bolero-type dance. I was dressed as a cowboy—but I didn't have Deanna Durbin in my arms; I did, however, have a six-shooter that fired caps. (Boy, did I cause a rumpus; finally, they had to take the gun away.)

The manicured gardens at the rear of the storybook mansion were the last resort for having fun; so, accompanied by my niece (Amelixis), nephew (José), and a few friends, we went out to play tag. We were careful not to get dirty because—if we did—we would get spanked. In one of my hysterical dashes to avoid getting tagged, I ran into the buffet room, slipped on the slick marble floor, slid and slammed into a three-tiered white cake, and got frosting all over myself and my costume. That was the end of my party! Mamá dragged me home by the ears and gave me a spanking for playing rough. The next thing that I remember—I was being flown to the USA and the wonderful state of Connecticut.

The Stroke of Life

I have so many wonderful memories of my childhood in Cuba that I could go on forever with these stories; for now, this is just a prelude for my trip back—my first visit to Cuba in more than half a century. After years of waiting for the opportunity to explore my roots, the moment had arrived for me to revisit my place of birth. In 1959 Cuba became a communist state and I was denied entry after that date. As a US citizen, it was illegal to travel to Cuba. Just recently, Cuban-born American citizens were allowed to travel to the island, as long as they had families still living there. I have several friends who visited by way of Cancún, México, and they all returned home safely; and since there were no direct flights from New York to Havana, I went to Cancún—using it as a "jumping-off" place to visit my island. Although I feared being discovered illegally in Cuba, I decided to take the risk and go.

After suffering a slight stroke the year before, I realized how fleeting life can be, so I vowed that I would not waste the rest of this life—no matter the cost. "God and country, please forgive me, but these are my desires and my adventure."

THE STORY: From JFK to Cancún, Destination Havana

It's Saturday, August 21st, 1999; the time is 3:00am. I'm having coffee, doing last minute packing and checking my documents. Due to long lines and inspections, the airports want passengers to arrive at least one and a half hours before take-off. (I'm as ready as I'll ever be.) It's now 4:30am and I'm waiting out on the sidewalk for the car service to pick me up, as scheduled. Twenty minutes passed and I had the feeling the car was not coming. I let two empty cabs go by and I was determined to take the third. It was getting late and I was getting upset. Not a cab in sight. I walked half a block to the corner—lugging a heavy bag—and tried my luck. I looked down both ends of the street and, surprisingly, there was no traffic—just a car here and there making turns, but nothing coming my way. I had no time to return home to call another company, so I stood there and prayed. I don't know whether the prayers had anything to do with it, but—within two minutes—a cab pulled up. It got me to the airport in plenty of time and I found out later that the private car never showed up.

The flight is scheduled for 7:10am, leaving from J.F.K. International airport on Aeroméxico to Cancún; I don't really remember the flight number, but it's already 7:45am and we haven't taken off; it also raining—maybe, that's the reason for the delay. After six months preparing for this trip to Cuba, it doesn't seem to be going as well as anticipated.

We're finally taking off now—at 8:00am and the estimated arrival time is three hours and fifty minutes. Hopefully, the plane will make up time in the air and get me there on schedule—so that I can make my connecting flight to Havana. This trip has been on hold since 1959 and I couldn't wait any longer. I'm not sure what to expect, but it will be an emotional experience; my mind was open to anything and everything. There are tropical storms hovering around Cuba—I hope they don't dampen my visit. I have always manage to travel in the rain; I guess it's a sign of soul cleansing.

We're flying above the clouds now; the sky is blue and it's clear up here. I wonder how I'll feel when I see those tall, beautiful palm trees swaying in the warm tropical breeze. They scared the hell out of me as a boy and, to this day, they still remind me of giant tarantula spiders—silhouetted on the sky, during a tropical sunset.

I'll probably cry when my plane descends towards the island—just like I did in 1971, when I flew over the southern tip of Cuba on a trip to Jamaica. It is all so emotional for me. My family thinks I'm crazy, but they remember more than I do—maybe, some bad times that they don't want to talk about. I remember huge, yellow-green plants; beautiful, multi-colored flowers; giant butterflies; the ocean sparkling like a million, white diamonds against the backdrop of an iridescent blue sea with a brilliant orange-colored sky. Although I was only a child then, I was blessed with an eye for beauty. I remember my house, and bathing with cool, clear rainwater, collected in a large barrel that sat in the backyard. We used a tin can or an old pan to pour the water. There was the playground, and the schoolhouse with the fruit trees that I climbed. I picture the park, with its promenade, where people gathered to socialize. I often think of the theater, the ice cream, and my favorite jukebox. These memories are never too far from my thoughts.

It seems that every time I travel alone, I get a whole row of seats to myself; I suppose the airlines want me to be extra comfortable. Well, it really doesn't happen all the time; but, here I am on the plane, facing the window, gazing at the clouds. Meanwhile, my mind is racing in anticipation with all these what-to-do thoughts: "while in Havana, I could visit with a cousin, however, since I'm only staying for a few days, I'm afraid this might take up valuable time." I need every precious second to explore my feelings and be with my own thoughts. I'm skeptical and afraid, but I'm sure I'll manage—as I live this adventure.

It was 11:30pm when I passed out last night to be awaken at 3:30am by the sound of a rooster's "cock-a-doodle-do"—my alarm-clock watch. (It will sound more appropriate in Cuba.) I didn't get much sleep—due to the excitement of the trip. I was hoping to sleep on the plane, as I usually do, but it didn't happen that way. I love children, but not when they're kicking the back of my seat, as I try to get some shut-eye. I waited for 15 minutes before reprimanding the little girl—and asking her to stop kicking the seat. She pouted and started to whimper and that's just what I needed—now, I had to put up with her screaming. The girl's mother, also spoiled, disliked my reproach, but she did make the kid stop. (Thank God.)

No longer sleepy, I reached for my 4x6 notepad, and started to enter my story—up to this moment. On my pad, I will record my daily activities, as they happen throughout the trip. I'm feeling nervous, and the thought of whether I will make the flight to Havana on time keeps me awake. Breakfast was a bowl of corn flakes, yogurt, coffee, and a stale cupcake. (If this plane crashes, I don't want this to be my last meal!) I'm getting a pain on the right side of my stomach—it must be indigestion. I ask the stewardess about the connecting flight and she assured me that I will make the shuttle, as scheduled—I'm not so nervous anymore.

This girl is a terror! Like I said before, "I love children." But on the way back, I hope there won't be any near me—so I can relax. I looked out the window, as a rain cloud shed its tears, followed by rays of colors. (I'm surely over the rainbow, now.)

We'll be touching down in 15 minutes—as we fly over México, the scenery below is radiant with blue-green water and coral reefs. There's a regatta of sailboats riding the waves and leaving whitewater trails behind. I'm also imagining all the vivid-colored species of fish underneath the lush aqua-green vegetation found in Cancún's coast.

Going through Mexican immigration is a breeze; but time marches on and I worry that I might not make the connection to Havana. I have to take a short walk out of the arrival building and into the departure building of *Cubana* Airlines. I'm in awe of how many people are headed for Cuba; I will surely miss my flight if I have to wait for all these people to check-in. I aggressively approach an attendant and show him my letter of introduction, written by my travel agent. He reads the letter and leads me to the front of the line, where I handed my passport and documents to the attendant—and waited impatiently. It took some time for them to find my visa among the scattered papers on the counter, but all was there. All my documents were in order. The friendly attendant at the counter happened to be a personal friend of my travel agent, and he gave me his personal card and instructed me on the delicate and safe procedures of traveling to Cuba. He's nice, but he's on *mañana* time and my nerves are getting shot. Thanks to the tranquilizers prescribed by my doctor, my blood pressure is under control and my nerves are holding steady.

After my bags were checked, I ran through a long corridor towards gate #10, where another security check awaited me. I didn't have a clue which way to go; but I kept asking for directions and finally made it to the gate—on time! There's so much intrigue, as they bus us to the airplane parked on the runway; I feel as if I'm in a scene from "Casablanca." I take a picture of the plane for posterity; next stop, Havana! I'm am like...so wired!

On board, there were no seating assignments; I just took whatever seat was available.

It's now 12:30pm and I'm finally on board the *Cubana* Airlines or Cuban territory. It's hot as hell inside, and packed with loud-speaking people, each greeting one another. (Meanwhile, I say "hello" to a fly resting on my hand.) My partner, Mike, would have killed it instantly—he hates flies with a passion. This fly was different though; it was a Cuban fly—so I let it live. There are lots of pretty people, both young and old, on board; by their enthusiasm, you knew they were visiting relatives they haven't seen in a very long time.

Next stop, Havana airport! ... where someone holding a sign with my name on it will escort me to the hotel.

I took a window seat, so that I could see Cuba from the air as we descended; and maybe take a picture. I noticed smoke coming up from between my legs. Now, I was getting really nervous and concerned; but nothing seemed to be burning. Later, I was told that condensation from the improvised cooling system was responsible for the smoke. The overhead lights don't work either; but fortunately, the motor does!

Siboney is playing in the background. "How appropriate," I thought. The plane is packed with tourists and it's 90° inside; everyone is perspiring heavily and the women are keeping cool by fanning themselves with whatever they can get their hands on; the air system and the lights on the overhead panel don't work well or not at all; there are broken seats in the first-class section stuck in a reclining position—I'm sitting in one of them. Considering the terrible shape the plane is in, I hope that we make it across the Gulf. I'm sure we will; I console myself, because I'm carrying the St. Christopher's medal in my pocket and he never lets me down. I also have many good wishes and blessings from my close friends. Mike is sitting on pins and needles, until he hears from me; he can't wait for this trip to end, so that I can be safe at home. Aeroméxico supplied us with peanuts and a glass of mango juice on ice. I wonder if I'll get "Montezuma's revenge," since the ice was loaded in Cancún. I won't think about it now—tomorrow's another day.

The pain in my side kicks in every so often and I can't pass gas; if I did, I'd kill everyone in first class. I won't—I'll wait until I'm on the ground—and the very first thing I'll do upon reaching Havana is pass gas! Although, at this point, I'm turning green.

Gazing out the window, I see huge puffy clouds—like the ones I remember from childhood—and just like they were drawn in my first grade school book. Near the shore, the water is a vivid turquoise. I can tell that we're traveling north on the western coast of Cuba, but I don't know where we are. I see narrow roadways and trails winding around the mountains—as well as lush, green meadows and farmland. The soil is the color red—evidence of rich copper depots.

Santería is still a way of life in Cuba. I see many people wearing beaded necklaces and bracelets that represent their chosen saints. The attendants are selling duty-free *Obatala* and *Changó* dolls, French perfume, and liquor. (The Saints are on sale.) I'm tempted to buy one, but I'm also afraid that bringing back a souvenir from Cuba would document this trip. ($10,000 and/or imprisonment is the penalty for any American citizen caught traveling to Cuba, without permission.)

As we start our descent into Havana, a nostalgic Rumba version of "Perhaps, Perhaps, Perhaps" is playing. It's a bumpy ride inside the white clouds. I think of JFK, Jr., and I imagine the terror he must have felt—staring out the cockpit window of his plane, not knowing if he's flying up or down. I hope my captain has more flying time than our American Prince—may he rest in peace.

Through a break in the clouds I can see Havana. We're flying low at this point and it looks like a great metropolis. As we land at *José Martí* International Airport, everyone applauds loudly. The drumbeat of the song, *Que Viva Changó*, in honor of an Afro-Cuban Saint, also known as *Santa Bárbara,* is booming from the loudspeakers. How appropriate; I can't believe I'm finally here! In CUBA! In the flesh! "Que viva, me!"

HAVANA:
At José Martí International Airport

Saturday, August 21st, 1:00pm. So far, I've had one hell of a trip. I'm emotionally and physically exhausted, and I can't wait to get to the hotél and take a long shower. At the airport, I passed inspection with flying colors. While in line to present my documents to the immigration officer, I noticed dogs everywhere—sniffing for drugs or whatever they're addicted to. One sniffed at my sneakers and ran an un-welcomed cold nose up my leg. We looked at each other and I apologized, "Sorry, but I haven't got what you're panting for." The dog gazed at me for a second, as if it understood, sneezed an acknowledgment, and walked away to sniff other bags. In relief, I muttered, "Bless you." (Cuban dogs are highly trained and bilingual; it must have something to do with Xavier Cugat's intellectual Chihuahuas.) I looked around sheepishly to see if anyone had been listening to my conversation with the dog.

It was now my turn to face the officer. He asked for my passport and visa, which I quickly handed him through an open slot underneath the glass window. Everything was in order, but he didn't stamp my passport. He looked at me and asked if I have a Cuban passport—which I also handed him. He looked at it in awe, then looked back at me, and said, "you haven't changed a bit." After all, he was looking at a picture of a 6-year-old boy, within an antique-quality passport, dated October 13, 1948—that's the year that I left Cuba. With a friendly smile, he called several attendants over to look at my passport—as this was something they hadn't seen before. I thought that I was in trouble—instead—I was an instant celebrity. They smiled and welcomed me home; I cautiously passed through the gates. I was finally in Cuba.

The baggage claim department was in chaos: bags were very slow coming in and I was losing my cool. "I'll just go with it; after all, it's the tropics and I've only been waiting 20 minutes; but it feels like an eternity, when you're anxious to get to the hotel." I looked around and saw a bag similar to mine in the distance; I'm thinking, "if it's off the carousel, then it must belong to someone else." I ignored it and kept watching for mine. Forty-five minutes passed and most passengers were already on their way out—except for me. The suitcase that I saw earlier was still there, so I went to inspect it; sure enough, it was mine. Someone must have taken it off the carousel and left it there; not very nice, the least they could've done was put it back on the carousel. Now, I'm angry! Then, another checkpoint, with two long lines of people waiting to present their baggage stubs. An impatient man decided to cut in front of my line; another man, standing in back of me, got angry and aggressively advised him to return to his own line. They exchanged words, tempers flared, there was lots of arm waving and—finally—the first man went back to his proper place in line. It was all bark and no bite: Cubans have no patience. The two men walked out friends—after glaring at each other with hateful eyes.

Outside the terminal, I was met by Havanatour personnel, who gave me the appropriate vouchers for my hotel stay in Havana and Varadero Beach, as well as the corresponding transfers to and from the airport and the hotels. I boarded the air-conditioned bus, which was waiting for 2 more passengers—who were late. The bus waited for 15 minutes and finally left—without them.

All this excitement is not for the weak at heart. The bus is rolling now and the next stop is the infamous *Hotel Nacional*—where I'll be staying for the next three nights. A short stay, you might say - for someone who hasn't inhaled Cuban air for half a century; but—by the end of this trip—I will have justified the reasons.

On the way to the hotel, Cary, the transfer operator, gave the passengers valuable information on how to see the city the right way: the use of money; cabs; gratuities; how to get around; and, most of all, how to keep safe. As we drove through Havana, the sights started to register in my mind—from having seen them in picture books and postcards. We passed *El Morro* Castle, and the famous *Malecón* Promenade, and many statues honoring my hero, *José Martí*. On the bus, looking out the window, it felt as if I was watching a movie. I must set my feet on solid ground to get a true sense of really being here and that this is all actually happening to me—right now.

The once-beautiful buildings that line the *Malecón* are now shabby and in desperate need of repair. Some areas remind me of London (after the blitz), or the shabby parts of San Juan, Puerto Rico, or the ghettos of the Bronx (only with a Spanish-European flavor). San Juan is still one of my favorite destinations; I guess it reminds me of home. Before getting off the bus, I booked a private tour of Havana with Cary. I'm still afraid to venture out alone; back home, friends had put fear in me by telling me horror stories about what could happen.

The bus pulled up to the *Hotel Nacional* and my bags were rushed to the registration desk. Papers are already in order, so I was escorted directly to my room: #763, on the 7th floor—overlooking parts of Havana, *El Malecón*, the never-ending sea, and the entrance to the hotel. I gave the bellboy an American dollar and he exuberantly thanked me—the exchange rate is 90 pesos to the dollar. There was no air-conditioning in the room and it was hot! The front desk attendant forgot to give me the plastic card that has to be inserted into a slot for the air conditioning to work, so I called down and a young man came up with the card—*pronto*. Unpacking was fast. I usually travel incredibly light—this time lighter than ever: 1 off-white suit; 4 pairs of underwear; 4 pairs of socks; 1 white shirt; 1 pair of safari shorts, with plenty of pockets; 4 tee-shirts, in assorted colors; 1 belt; 2 swim suits; 1 swim cap, with goggles; my toiletries; a pair of brown dress shoes; beach sandals; and, a shoulder bag for my cameras. The carry-on bag was all that I needed; my suit is pressed, so I was set for the week. Now, it's time for that long-awaited shower to get the travel dust off my body—and start enjoying my vacation.

The *Hotel Nacional* is a true landmark: the playground of the "rich and famous"—visited by celebrities from all over the globe and—now—me!

After exploring the interior of the hotel—with its fine restaurants and shops—I strolled out to the garden—surrounded in tropical splendor, with an awesome view of the ocean. There was a wedding taking place and pictures were flashing. Guests were drinking on the balcony and resting on wicker rocking chairs; tropical birds-of-paradise sang gently; peacocks and pheasants strolled freely on the manicured grounds; the distant song of a rooster suddenly reminded me of the talking watch that—back home—awakens me at eight o'clock every morning. Without warning, a huge thunderhead covered the sky and all Havana turned an ominous, dark gray. The loud, rolling thunder shook the earth; then a crack of lightening, and the threat of torrential rains made everyone run for cover. Once inside the hotel, I sat gazing out to sea, watching nature's floor show. The rain came down hard and the ocean tides swelled high—making the waves crash violently against the *Malecón* wall and spilling water onto the streets. The traffic came to a complete halt for a short time and when the excitement and fear of the storm was over, everything was peaceful once more and the partying continued—as if nothing had happened.

All this excitement made me mighty hungry; so, I made my way down to the restaurant for a buffet dinner. I didn't want to chance a la carte dining—just in case I didn't like the food; at least with the buffet, I have a choice. The host greeted me at the door and showed me the food that was available; then, he introduced me to the cook and the boy in charge of decorating the tables. They were so proud of their handiwork. I didn't have the heart to tell them that I've seen better decorations; but I gave them five stars for effort. On the menu was what I wanted and longed for—seasoned pork, rice and beans, yucca in garlic sauce, crispy pork rinds, flan for dessert, and a cup of good Cuban coffee (*café con leche*). After eating all that, you can put me out to pasture for a *siesta*.

As I feasted, I was interrupted several times by the cook and the decorator, who anxiously asked questions about New York City and the outside world. Not that they're unaware of what's going on outside of Cuba; in fact, they're very well informed. They just like to hear it fresh from the people they meet. I declined an invitation—for later that evening—to attend a house party to continue our conversation and perhaps do a little more bonding, but I was completely exhausted and I wanted to retire early and get as much rest as possible. I've had a long day and Cary was picking me up at 9:00am for the city tour. I tipped generously and they were grateful and gracious. Before leaving the dining room, the female trio that had been playing guitar and singing nostalgic songs of yesteryear appeared before my table and I couldn't escape. After listening to three notable songs, I thanked and tipped them—walking out with a cassette recording of their rendition of famous Cuban love songs—as a souvenir.

Back in the lobby, I passed by a poster announcing the 10 o'clock show at the Parisian Club. It was right here and I didn't have to go out and get wet. It was only 9:30pm and I decided that it was too early to get 'horizontal.' After all, it's Saturday night and I was in Cuba. The club was packed and I was seated with a gentleman from México, who came to Cuba periodically to look at the pretty girls. Shame on the old man—he must've been at least 80 years old! He must've also been taking Viagra or some kind of Mexican stimulant. At first, he seemed not to want company, but he had no choice; he was alone and so was I—and I wanted the front row seat. After I charmed him with my knowledge of México, he settled down and became more engaging. A few drinks later, he became friendlier, and—by show time—I was dealing with a drunken old man, dribbling from the mouth and slurring his words. I totally ignored him, but I must confess, I couldn't wait for the show to end and lose this character.

The Las Vegas-like review had attractive singers and dancers and lasted for two hours; numerous costume changes and production numbers hit the stage, one after another, without interruption. Exciting mulatto women, topless and scantily clad in colorful feathers from birds-of-paradise, paraded on stage. These beautiful, brown women popped every man's eyes and were the envy of the women watching the show. I was enchanted watching them dance for two non-stop hours. It was definitely time to get to bed.

It's 1:00am and I know I won't have any trouble falling asleep. *Mojitos* were the drink of this evening and I was very brave in consuming four. I shall sleep like a baby, without interruption; obviously, I was brain dead from the effects of the 100% proof rum. Not a single dream appeared in my blank mind. "Surely," I thought, "one good nightmare would have been great!"

I was awakened by my next-door neighbor yelling, "will you please kill the rooster." My "Rooster Alarm Watch" had gone off at 7:00am—as programmed—but it failed to wake me up. (I was out cold.)

I got up with a pounding head, made my way to the window and opened the curtains. What a glorious morning: Havana is coming to life and its people are going to work; the taxicabs are lining up in front of the hotel to take tourists on their journeys; bike drawn rickshaws are making their way to the old part of town—to be used as taxis on the narrow streets; the sun is shining bright on a cloudless sky; this is a great day for a city tour. Cary was picking me up at 9:00am, so I had to rush...clean up...have breakfast...and make myself ready for her. I was already running a half hour late.

Papaya, mango, fried eggs, bacon, sweet rolls, and coffee—what a way to start the day! As I dashed out of the hotel, I met my neighbor and apologized for my noisy rooster. He completely understood: "You're in Havana, my friend," he said. "I sat near you last night at the club and you were feeling no pain, have a nice day."

The Tour

Without a moment to lose, I ran down to the corner to meet Cary, who was standing next to a small, red, beat-up car—and wearing a big smile. After a warm hello and a morning hug, she introduced her friend, Tony, as the man who would drive us around town. Inside the car, she also introduced me to another young man—also named Tony, except that this Tony was far away from his home, Australia. A sophisticated traveler in his early 20's, he carried a camera in one hand and a camcorder over his shoulders. With wavy, brown hair, black sun glasses a la 'men in black,' a little fuzz on his chin, and a ring on his thumb, Tony was determined to take a piece of Cuba back home with him—on cellophane. He was older beyond his years; worked as a computer programmer; and, was interested in travel, fine arts, great food, and beautiful women.

Tony, the driver, was very much a typical Cuban: 30-something, dark curly hair; fast talking with a great sense of humor; always joking, patting you on the back, and looking straight into your eyes with a warm and friendly grin. And, of course, decorating his upper lip was a mustache. He knew how to make a buck.

Cary was sensitive, fragile—she reminded me of the comic book

19

character, "Nancy." She wore her dark hair in a chin length bobbed haircut, with straight bangs covering her brow, reflected a warm and caring personality, and was smart as a whip. Cary knew Cuban history better than any professor on the island; she had an answer to every question.

We spent the entire day walking on cobblestones, visiting the major sights and sounds of Havana—until the heat of the day wore us down.

At the tour's end, I invited Cary and Aussie Tony to a coffee break and a chance to capture a little air conditioning. At the Café, we had a chance to bond with each other and speak frankly about the government and its politics. Cary confessed that the Cuban people are ready for a major change; they realize now that this regime no longer works without the help of a major power to support it—and—they feel—that it never did, right from the start. They, the people, are urged to wait until something better comes along. The dream was just an illusion; the promise of a better life and equality was never fulfilled; a large percentage of the population still goes to bed hungry and Cary feared for her children's future. I was so overwhelmed by Cary's story and the hardship that the Cuban people are experiencing that I began to weep. Cary's tears pooled in her eyes and Tony also reflected sadness in silence. Before departing, we promised to write to each other and—with melancholy hearts—said "*adiós.*"

The day was ending too soon and there were still many sights to see and things to do. With this in mind, Aussie Tony and I continued our adventure and returned to the old city. I wanted Cuban pastries and he wanted cigars. He was thin and I was chubby...guess why? Passing by *La Casa de la Paella* restaurant, hunger pangs signaled for food and Paella was the way to go—with a Corona 'n' lime chaser. We bonded some more and made plans to meet later that evening—to see the show at the world-famous *Tropicana* Nightclub. I had purchased my ticket in advance, which included transportation, so Tony would have to go solo; but not before going to *El Morro* Castle, for the firing of the cannons—a ceremony held every night at 9:00pm to announce that all was well. The show at the "Trop" started at 10:00pm, so we had to leave soon after the "big bang." With these plans in hand, we departed for our hotels to freshen up for the nighttime extravaganza, and to wait for Tony, the driver, to pick us up and take us to the hill, where the firing took place.

It's 6:30pm and the threat of rain was evident as the dark clouds began to gather. "If it rains, the show at the "Trop" will be cancelled and I will be extremely disappointed to have come all this way and not see the famous show—after years of anticipation."

Before Tony, the driver, retrieves us from our respected hotels and delivers us to *El Morro* for the big "Boom," what I anticipated happened: it started to pour cats and dogs, and—again—the rolling thunder and crackling lights made their presence known. Aussie Tony, convinced that the show would be cancelled, did not show up at our meeting place. Now, I'm stranded with no "Boom" and possibly no "Trop." I had no way to get in touch with Aussie Tony, so I decided to go my own way; he knew where I'd be later—if it ever stops raining. I will—most likely—see him there.

During my dinner at the hotel, the rain came to a halt, as quickly as it had begun, and promptly at 9:00pm, the bus to the cabaret was loaded with happy tourists.

The mansions on "Fifth" are remnants of a rich past—once own by doctors, lawyers, and the very wealthy. The homes are now all in need of immediate renovation. The walls are crumbling and crying out for paint; but, paint in Cuba is very expensive and of very bad quality. Only the large modern hotels, which are primarily own by Spaniards, are able to acquire quality paints and building materials—for the sake of the paying tourists.

Spain seems to be taking over Cuba, just like Christopher Columbus did in 1492. Meanwhile, Castro boosts the Cuban economy by heavily taxing the foreign conglomerates. Spain is joined by Canada, Germany, France, Argentina, México, and, most of the free world, in modernizing and conducting business in Castro's Cuba—which reaps the wealth from the tourists' money—including the dollars sent by Cubans living in America, who send money to their families in order to fund their well being. America is not represented in Cuba in any way, shape, or form—and, on this island, which is a mere 90 miles away. The US embargo is only hurting the people, who have been blindly deceived; it's not hurting the Cuban government. Castro is a hardheaded man, fully aware that the revolution did not and is not achieving its desired purpose. Castro is willing to go to his grave as the last revolutionary communist—before admitting that he is wrong. Cuba is the key to our shores; it's time we save her.

The Tropicana Nightclub

I saw hundreds of twinkling lights shining through the trees—as we approached the *Tropicana* Club—the garden was filled with red and yellow flowers, nestled in the dense tropical foliage leading to the entrance—the fountain, with its dancing waters which constantly changed colors, was magical—the sweet fragrance of the wet soil played with my senses. As one entered the theater, men were given a cigar and the women a red rose. It's sad that Native Cubans never get to see their homeland's famous show; this is due to the hefty price tag for a seat, $65 dollars—which will feed a family of five for 4 months—maybe 6 months—if spread thin. The club was filling up fast—with tourists from all over the world. I heard different languages—besides Spanish—being spoken, as people passed by; the revelers were seated as quickly as the club's employees could dry the rain-soaked chairs and tables. It was exciting to watch the hustle, bustle, and confusion necessary—to prepare the stage for show time. It's was like watching the raising of a circus tent—everyone pulling together—animals included.

I was quickly seated (ringside of course) and I waited for a long time for the liquor set-up to arrive. The club's setting is conducive to drinking and I wanted a cocktail—*pronto*. While waiting for the drinks, I entertained myself by searching for Aussie Tony—a guppy among the sea of people—which was almost an impossible task. I had figured that by casually scanning the room, without actually making an effort to look for him, he would suddenly appear. I was dying of thirst and getting thirstier by the seconds; I was getting a sneaking suspicion that my drink was coming by way of Canada. (What is taking so long?)

A noisy group of friendly, fun-loving, young people were seated at my table. We exchanged jokes and recommended other activities worth doing on the island, which drew my attention away from the booze I was craving. We were all on a fake high—because no one had a drink to initiate the evening.

The orchestra was starting to tune-up and, finally, the waiter brought the drinks. We're seven at the table; I'm the odd man out and we have three bottles of run to share among us—with a bottle of ginger ale, a club soda, a cola, and some kind of a lemon soda—which no one touched. Oh, yes!—also, a bucket of ice.

The lights are slowly dimming; the spectacle is about to begin. Everyone rushes to their seats; the audience quiets down; the orchestra blares the first notes of introduction. A puff of red and yellow smoke engulfs the immense tri-level stage. The dancers perform in a 360 degree environment, so you don't know from which side they'll be entering—until one of them taps you on the shoulder and dedicates a song to you. Four groups of ballerinas appear on the stage, dressed in iridescent blue; then another group in green; another in red; yet another in white. The show girls (or models) are carefully picked by the dance captain for their beauty and perfection of body; they are non-dancers. These girls parade in beautiful, elaborate, and dazzling costumes that glitter in the night sky. They wear enormous feathered hats or headdresses made from the feathers of birds-of-paradise and they look absolutely unreal. These dancers make a grand entrance— to the anonymous approval of the audience, who begin to applaud loudly and wildly. More singers, dancers, and acrobats fill the stages; it's like a 3-ring circus, because no one knows where to look first. At the same time, topless girls parade near the tables, wearing a four foot high chandelier on their head that actually lights up; this is a major highlight of the show and is performed every night. It's a landmark production. The house lights go out and the club is in total darkness. One chandelier lights up from the far corner of the room, another lights up on the other end—then another—and another—and another—and so on—and so on. Meanwhile, you're surrounded by beautiful, topless, twinkling chandelier women, dancing to the latest salsa beat. It's a beautiful sight and the audience goes bananas. More beauties ascend from beyond the trees. The women seem to be dropping out of the sky; dancing with pageantry, they retell the story of the discovery of Cuba—with the fashions and religious beliefs of the time—all through the art of mime, song, dance, and outrageous costumes.

In order to make this show work, the club must employ a family of at least 200 people; this includes cooks, porters, bartenders, waiters, and everything between. I say family, because I know—from experience—that everyone has to get along and pitch in—to help, when someone else is in trouble or sick. In showbiz, there's no such thing as "I did more than he or she did, etc." Everyone helps one another unconditionally—following a certain rhythm or pattern every night—

23

the same way—or else it doesn't work.

The rapid movements of the strobe lights, combined with special effects, were making me rather dizzy—of course, the four rum 'n' cokes I easily managed to consume also helped with the weakening of my brain; not only the dancers were dancing, the audience was too.

With my slurred vision, I spotted Aussie Tony: sitting ringside, smoking the Cuban cigar that he got at the entrance (that looked bigger than he was), and downing a rum 'n' coke—one of his many, I was sure.

I joined Tony's table—also shared by a Spaniard and his Cuban girl friend; it was just a matter of time before we'd find one another. Tony introduced me to his new friends and we drank some more, in celebration of life. The Spaniard and his girl friend—a happy, devil-may-care, kind of couple—he lives in Spain and she, in Cuba—both were madly in love with each other; but, as the saying goes, "so close and yet so far away." The show was wrapping up the grand finale and Tony looked a bit sick; I escorted him to the rest room and—fifteen minutes later—he emerged a new man. He was so sick his tan turned grey—remember Pinocchio, when he smoked the cigar and drank all the booze and turned green—as well as grew Donkey ears? Well, do I need say more.

After the show, the orchestra played for the dancing pleasure of the guests and, since we were 3 sheets to the wind, and dancing alone is acceptable in this modern day, Tony and I decided to get up and dance—making our unannounced debut—on the world famous *Tropicana* stage.

After making total fools of ourselves, our new found friends invited us to join them for drinks at the *Havana Café* at the plush Riviera Hotel. When we arrived, the outrageous salsa orchestra, The *Van Vans* was playing to a massive crowd of music lovers.

Havana Café

The *Havana Café* faces the vast open waters—towards Florida. There, we encountered a long line of anxious dancers, waiting to be let in—reminiscent of the glory days of NYC's Studio 54. Our new friends—who I'll never see again—were staying at the hotel and used this influence to get us into the club; twenty five dollars later, we entered the dark, smoky, overcrowded room. I'm sure it was a fire hazard, but we're in Cuba. It's party time in the playground of the world—which Cuba still is—in a roundabout way.

Los Van Van, the current and notorious salsa band was tearing up the dance floor—playing their latest hits. Eight musicians and two singers were making sounds the music world envies—hips were swaying and arms were waving over our heads—everyone on the dance floor swung to the salsa rhythm of the tropics. In an attempt to get a drink, Tony and I inched our way towards the bar; but, before getting there, two lovely women dragged me by the arm onto the dance floor and soon disappeared in pursuit of other bodies. Needless to say, I never left the crowded dance floor; I danced with everyone—men, women, broomsticks—but mostly, like everyone else, by myself and, with the best partner in the house, "The Music."

My three new friends finally joined me on the dance floor and brought me a welcomed bottle of ice cold beer—we danced nonstop—to near exhaustion—until the wee hours of the morning. Tired, drunk, and drenched in perspiration, I knew I had to make my exit—that is, if I were to have "later this very morning" a full and productive day. (It's already today!)

I said my farewell to everyone; Tony and I agreed to exchange photographs and stay in touch by the internet. Tony planned leaving the following day for Los Angeles to become a movie star; but, if the movies don't pan out, before heading home to Australia, he'll try to break the bank in Las Vegas. We have the same dreams—wonderful dreams.

I took a cab—dragging my limp and abused body to sleep. Lights O.....U.....T.....thank you! "Thank you, God of the universe, for such a wonderful day."

The Next Day

I was startled when the "rooster" alarm went off at 7:00am; if it'd been a real bird—and a few hundred years back in time—I would have gladly sacrificed it to the gods. While stumbling in the dark, trying to find the damn watch, I bumped my head on the night table and fell to the floor. I wanted to stop the "crowing", before the man next door started banging on the wall again. (I had gone to bed at 3:00a.m.—with my head feeling like the size of a basketball—and I forgot to reset the watch for at least an hour later.)

I staggered to the window and opened the curtains—to let the bright sun into the room, hoping that it will eventually wake me. "Ah, there you are, you blasted watch. Run out of batteries, did you? I guess I'll have to replace them; you are all I got."

It was time to exercise and burn off those extra calories that I've gained during these past few days of indulging in fine drink and food. With only four hours of sleep, I'm still determined to have a vigorous workout—before breakfast—to stimulate the ole' body. Lazily, I got my swimming gear together and made my way—blindly—to the pool. I dove bravely—head first—into the cool water and my body was instantly refreshed. "Or, am I having a stroke? I don't know anything; I'm still asleep."

I was shivering from the morning breeze. I had goose bumps all over my body, like a turkey's skin after the feathers have been plucked. It was much warmer under the water, so I kept myself under, for as long as it took—for my body to acclimate. Looking up towards the surface—from the bottom of the pool—I saw the morning star shining through the ripples of the water. I love lying on the bottom of the pool; I get to feel like I have drowned. "What an awful thought this early in the morning!" All I have to do is let the air out of my lungs and I drop right to the bottom. "Don't attempt this alone, though—it's dangerous."

I was serious about exercising and swam for thirty minutes—breaking the morning silence with the splashing of water. I thought myself a dolphin, cutting through water at incredible speed and swimming elegantly, like Flipper—knowing, all the while, that I looked more like Orca, the killer whale, doing belly flops.

I felt energized after my workout and I was eager to start the day. My head—numb from the night before—was slowly returning to normal and I was ready for some heavy nourishment. I was too wet to sit inside, so I ordered breakfast by the pool. It was quiet and peaceful—with a soft, warm breeze blowing—drying my swimsuit; besides, there were a few birds gathering to share my meal. "I can't let them down, can I?" Friendly little things—they fearlessly ate from my hands and we had a fine breakfast together. I bonded with my fine-feathered friends, as I daydreamed about the day's activities. "Hey! Bring back my toast!"

Regla

I needed to go to the town of *Regla*, but I had no idea how to get there. I called the front desk and asked them for directions; they suggested that I call a cab—and that's what I did. The taxi could only take me as far as the boat landing—where I boarded the ferry to cross Havana Bay to *Regla*. Standing in the crowded terminal, among many Afro-Cubans dressed in white and wearing colorful beaded necklaces and bracelets, I met a woman and her grandmother. We spoke about the freedom of religion that they now—somewhat—have in Cuba. It seems that Cubans can worship whichever God they want—and conduct their own ceremonies—without falling prey to the government. "Perhaps," the Pope's visit to Cuba did make a significant difference.

The ferry docked and people were getting off; there were as many bicyclists getting out, as there were waiting to get on—60% of the people boarding have bikes. It's the only means of free transportation that doesn't use gasoline—and a great way to stay fit.

Before I boarded the ferry, the lady that I met earlier asked me if I had the correct change for the ride. The fare to cross the bay is 10 cents—Cuban money—each way. I didn't have small change; I showed her a quarter and she said it was way too much money. Not wanting to give Castro more than his share, she offered to pay my fare—both ways. I felt like a child, so I offered her the quarter—which she didn't take—so I graciously thanked her. I watched her as she walked away and thought to myself, "Cubans are very generous people, even when they're in need."

The boat was filled to capacity—one more person on board and it would probably have sunk. Considering all the bikes on board, no one

27

got harassed. Everyone had his or her spot and were all busy balancing to the wobble of the boat. As I left Havana behind, I looked out to admire the wonderful view of Havana's Harbor. It took twenty five minutes to cross the bay—and we were docking in the town of *Regla*.

The first African slaves were brought to Cuba around 1510; by the 1520's, more than 4,000 slaves were being transported annually. The slaves were primarily taken from the Mandingo, Hausa, and Yoruba people of Africa. These Africans had a religion—which we now call *Santería*—that they were not allowed to practice in Cuba. It was not until much later that Afro-Cubans were able to observe their original religious traditions.

Back then, Cuba was a Spanish-ruled Catholic nation—that is until 1836, when some of the African people discovered the island across the Bay of Havana and settled the town of *Regla*. Here, the Africans founded the secret society of *Abacuá*—to worship their own gods.

As I walked towards the town, I had a strange feeling that every person who looked at me could read into my distant past—or see a future happening—or know of a mysterious moment in the now. The people from *Regla* are known to possess special powers that allow them to read your life; I tried not to make eye contact, in order to avoid a confrontation. I walked along a cobblestone road and the sound of drums playing started to beat in my mind. There were women seated by the roadside, dressed in white, selling religious articles: black voodoo dolls in colorful attire, incense, cologne, rattlers, and books. Statues of the many saints that they worship were also on display.

Everyone was looking at me; they knew that I was a stranger—a new face in town. I thought happy thoughts—just in case, they were able to read my mind. I stopped to ask for directions at the small church that housed *La Virgin de Regla*. There were 3 women standing by the door of the church and each one gave me a different direction; I chose the nearest one. It was a short mile away, next to the railroad tracks, on *Martí* road—that was easy to remember.

It was now twelve noon and unbearably hot; no shade could be found anywhere. Perspiration was running down my face—like if I was in a steam room. I tried not to think about the heat; I tried to concentrate on the town and my purpose for being here.

The buildings in *Regla* are one or two stories high, rarely three. The cobblestone road have many potholes, which have been filled with water from a recent downpour. I wish it would rain right now—to cool me off, while I'm on this hunt for the 12" piece of wood that's cut from a particular tree and used for a *Santería* ceremony. I passed homes with open doors and I couldn't help myself to look inside. Most were dark and poorly furnished, but they all had a refrigerator, a radio, and a television set. It seems everyone had a statue of a virgin placed on a pedestal on the wall or on a corner table dedicated exclusively to her—and decorated with flowers, lit candles, a glass of water, fruit offerings, the scent of *Agua Florida*, and, in some cases, a shot of rum and a cigar placed on top of a glass of water. "Why shouldn't these people worship the way they want?" I asked myself. "This is the cradle of the 'Secret Society.' It's their right." Again, the sound of drums was playing in my mind—a little bit more intense than before. I felt my blood pressure rising—from the exhausting heat of the sun. I was in such a hurry this morning—to start the day—that I forgot to take my medication.

I continued the hunt for the magic stick, through the rundown part of *Regla*, I could smell the different odors of the neighborhood, just like an animal smells its prey. The scent of a strong perfume from a recent *Santería* ceremony overwhelmed me. I sat on a park bench in the town's square—to rest my eyes for a while—I dozed off and started to daydream.....

I dreamt of being captured by a radical group and taken to a sacrificial place in the woods. The drums played as they tied me to a tree and placed candles and fruits at my feet. Drums are violently beating, as the voodoo priest takes a mouth full of rum and dances around me—suddenly, without warning, he spits the rum all over my face. He's wearing white parts and no shirt, with a red scarf around his neck. He's blowing smoke from a cigar and shakes the maracas around my body; he makes grunting noises—I watch in horror. My heart is pounding so hard that I swear everyone can hear it beating. I'm defenseless and I'm sure this is the end. He starts to blow cigar smoke in my face; I'm intoxicated from the smoke and I'm trying desperately to escape. My wrists are burning and bleeding from struggling with the ropes. A white chicken is sacrificed; its head is cut off and its blood poured over my head and body. I feel the warm blood run down my face and into my mouth. The stench of the bloody animal penetrates my senses—making me vomit. The drums are playing very loud now, and my heart is pounding harder and harder. They danced around me endlessly, hitting me with branches from a tree and chanting wildly—while others threw chicken feathers, which stick to the blood that covered my body. I'm was totally exhausted and dizzy with intoxication; I'm slowly giving up the fight. I have no more strength; my body is going limp. I can't keep my head up any longer—the drums are beating uncontrollably...LOUDER...LOUDER. The Voodoo priest walked slowly towards me, weaving from side to side—like a cat on the prowl—menacing me with a large machete—like the ones used to cut sugarcane. My eyes shut tightly and my lids got heavier and heavier; I surrender...what else can I do? I know this is the end and I silently pray to my God to keep my soul. The priest is in my face—so close, that I feel his decaying breath. I smelled the Devil. For the last time, I opened my eyes to gaze into the bloodshot eyes of Satan and witnessed his beastly snarl—but before his hand crushes and digs through my chest, tearing the heart out of my trembling body, I raised my head and gazed towards the sky and gave a final scream of terror. I saw him holding my still-beating heart—bleeding—in the palm of his hands.

Señor!...Señor!...Hey mister, wake up...are you all right? I'm startled by one of the ladies from the church, who shook me to consciousness. She was walking by the park and saw me asleep on the bench; thinking the worst, she came to my rescue. I thanked her for her concern and shared my dream. "You have fear in your eyes," she said. "You don't have to be afraid, you're with your own people now." I looked at her, smiled—and gently shook her hand.

The Santero's Store

I finally found the store I was looking for—next to the railroad tracks. I passed by and looked in discretely; it was a small, one-room store. One wall was filled w th tree branches with green leaves—like the ones I saw in my "day-mare." On the opposite wall was a rack with dissimilar-shaped pieces of wood, which were labeled and kept separate from each other—each piece of wood serves a different purpose for the practitioner. Getting my courage up, I approached the big man— sitting on a stool—sorting twigs on the floor. "Good afternoon" I said. "*Buen día*," he replied—as if I've been there before—"what can I get for you today?" I told him that I was searching for two pieces of wood, both twelve inches long and in the shape of the number 7. The name of the first piece was *Yamao*, the second was called *Jala Jala*. He only had the first piece available, the other was too difficult to get. He said that he had to travel fa′ and very deep into the forest to find the right branches, which grew way up on top of trees—far from easy reach. It has been six months since anyone in this area had seen this special twig. I guess one twig was better then none; at least, I wouldn't go home empty handed. He charged 30 centavos—about 8 American cents—for the twig. In New York, it would sell for at least $10, so I gave him double his price. "You're not from here, are you? He asked. I said, "No, I'm from America." He shook his head in approval. "God Bless" he said. "Have a safe trip back; come again soon."

There was a woman and a young man—quietly sorting bags of herbs and spices, and placing them on the wall. I asked them to pose for a picture—so that I could document my visit here. They were happy to oblige and I promised to send them a copy. On the way back to the ferry, I stopped at a store and bought a cookie that looked like the ones my father used to make. To my disappointment, it didn't taste the same, but I ate it anyway. A second lady from the church approached me and asked if had found what I was looking for; I said, "Yes"—and thanked her for her interest. They knew I was a stranger in these parts and were anxious to help me. I looked around one last time and spotted two dogs on a rooftop—marching back and forth, like prison guards peering down at the people. They assured me that I was still in a communist country.

Getting Back to Havana

On the way back to the ferry, I passed by the old church, and I decided to pay my respects to the Virgin, and leave a donation. The door was closed, so I knocked hard on the weathered, paint-chipped 18th century wooden door that didn't make a sound, due to its thickness. I looked around and found an old iron doorknocker; I gave the door two good knocks and, on the third try, the knocker fell off and bounced into a hole by the steps of the church. What luck! My hand fitted in the hole and I was able to retrieve it—but I didn't know what lived down there—waiting for some foreign food; so, I left a note on the door explaining what had happened and went on my way.

There were about 40 people waiting at the ferry landing. I took my place in line—under the canopy that shielded us from the sun. Everyone was perspiring heavily from the heat, and wiping their faces with red handkerchiefs.

Santa Bárbara is identified by the color red; half the population of Cuba is devoted to her. She's the goddess of thunder and lightning. Also known by her African name, *Changó*, she's considered a warrior—and she's used for both good and evil.

The women's penciled eyebrows were melting; not a breeze was blowing. Everyone wanted to get under the canopy to escape the heat—unaware that many bodies clustered together generated more heat, which made us hotter and more restless. I was devastated, waiting for the ferry; it must have just left the pier, prior to my getting there. I tried to think of things cold, to mentally bring my temperature down—before getting a heat stroke. I pictured myself in Aspen, Colorado—skiing down a beautiful glade of white powder snow, and the cold, icy wind blowing on my face. I was having a great time skiing, like I've never skied before, when the whistle of the ferry—upon arriving at the landing—shattered my award-winning race down the slippery Colorado hill. I didn't want to leave my imaginary mountain, but it was time to get back to reality and board the ferry. I rushed in and placed myself by a window—to feel, at least, a whisper of a breeze, as we cross the Bay. Others had the same intentions, but not all were successful.

"Hi there! Nice to see you again, can I share your window?" asked a lady from the church—who was standing behind me. "Certainly," I said. I told her about my incident at the church and she smiled. "That door knocker falls off all the time" she said. "But never into the hole. That's no problem, I'll get someone to retrieve it, when I get back," she laughed. "I'm the caretaker and I was taking a shower when you knocked on the door." We talked for the duration of the ride and she pointed out more interesting sights to discover.

The nice lady from the church mentioned a small town called *Casablanca*, which harbors a giant statue of Christ that can be seen from across the Bay. I imagined it to be a nice place to visit, but time was running out and there was much I wanted to do in Old Havana. Sometimes, I have to revisit a place to assure myself that I was really there. Today, I was on my own and I wanted a repeat performance of what I did yesterday—more daiquiris at the *Floridita* bar—and to devour more rich Cuban pastries.

La Capital

I strolled to the Capitol building and walked up the many stairs that lead to a massive steel doorway. The Capitol building was closed. From the top of the Capitol stairs, the panoramic view of the city was a sight to behold. The reconstructed government buildings looked very handsome and majestic, while the old apartment houses—with their balconies filled with green flowering plants—made the crumbling buildings look almost pretty. I rested on a bench in Central Park—facing a white statue of *José Martí* surrounded by towering palm trees—to contemplate the hustle and bustle of people walking, bicycling, children playing, and the 1950's vintage cars passing by. The intense heat of the day had passed and it was quite pleasant now. There was a slight breeze blowing and I was beginning to feel tired and sleepy.

The H. Upmann Tobacco Factory

I snapped out of my coma, and was energized once again. I wandered beyond the Capitol building and, at the back of this imposing building, I discovered the H. Upmann Tobacco Factory. You could smell the scent of fresh tobacco a block away. I don't smoke anymore, but I was compelled to enter the large, red building—which housed 3 floors of expensive, brown, addictive, tobacco leaves. I did a little investigating—for the sake of nostalgia; I once enjoyed smoking in my younger years, but now I choose not to. I took a quick tour of the factory and watched the expert hands pick, place, roll, and cut these wonderful cigars—considered to be the best throughout the world. I'm tempted to buy a couple of cases—as gifts to friends back home—but I'm afraid that customs will confiscate them in México. Plus, it will also document my trip. Still, I bought a *Romeo y Julieta*—which is my choice of cigar. I guess I just like the name; I'm a romantic at heart. Also available were *Cohíba* and *Hoyo de Monterrey*. It was very quiet inside the gift shop, as everyone sniffed and rolled the cigars to their ears—checking for fragrance and firmness. You'd think they were selling diamonds and pearls! It did remind me of the Baccarat tables at Trump's Casino in Atlantic City—where only the cards do the talking.

I left the cigar building, walked to the corner, and looked both ways. I looked to the left, "hmmmmm.....I already know what's down that way." I peered to the right, "hmmmmm.....that way seems very interesting." So.....I followed 'the yellow brick road' leading to Chinatown.

Chinatown

The scene in Chinatown changed from black and white to Technicolor. It reminded me of Dorothy, when she opened the door of her house and took her first glimpse of the enchanted world of OZ. Red and yellow buildings, with green and purple trimmings, lined the narrow streets. It was a maze of cobblestone alleys, with small gift shops and dirty restaurants. I love Chinese food and I was working up an appetite, but what I saw bottled on the counters was not so appetizing. Pickled pig snout, ears, and curly tails were not what I had in mind for dinner. The restaurants were very inviting, but also very dirty. Pretty girls, dressed in Chinese costumes, beckoned you to enter their near-empty establishments; but I no longer had an appetite.

People were gathering at a small square and I ran to observe the fun. (Most cities have their own "crazies" performing on street corners; Cuba is no exception.) There was a Chinese man with a homemade contraption, made up of different musical instruments attached together. He was dressed in a peasant costume, with flashing lights, and played the drums and cymbals, a car horn, and a tambourine—all while blowing on the harmonica. Everybody loved him. Me too—I gave him a big tip for the entertainment and went on my way.

An Art Exhibition

The day ended quickly and there was much more I wanted to see and do. Time is my enemy at this point; I must return to the hotel early enough to pack for my trip to Varadero Beach. This was my last night in Havana—until maybe, next year. I started walking to the hotel, which was two miles away, but a flea market near the promenade grabbed my attention. Local artists were exhibiting their works, done in oil and acrylic paintings, and sculptures, along with hand-crocheted baby clothing, and homemade toys. Some vendors were a bit aggressive trying to sell their crafts; but as soon as I mentioned that I'm Cuban, they left me alone.

An attractive woman approached me and introduced me to her 13-year old daughter. "She's pretty, no?" she said—with a heavy accent. "She is pretty, yes," I replied, knowing what she was up to. As I turned away, the woman grabbed my arm and asked, "You want, mister?" ..... "No, I don't want, thank you!" I said firmly—looking into her eyes with displeasure. "Why do you do this to this young girl; don't you know what God did to *Sodom and Gomorrah?*"..... "I know what the Bible says mister, but we have to make ends meet," she said—in Spanish. "I don't need you to preach to me, I know my sins and I'm not proud of them.....don't you think it doesn't hurt me to see my child walk into a room with a stranger, who I know will hurt and abuse her?.....It hurts mister, it hurts bad.....But, it's the only way we know." I hit a soft spot and had insulted her; she tearfully walked away—yelling, "Do you know your sins, mister?" ..... "Well, do you?" I stood there, solid as a rock—wanting to follow her to apologize. She was right; I had no business preaching to her. Who am I to judge others? Why should I care? If this is the only way for them to stay alive, then so be it. I'm not saying it's wrong, but it ain't right—I know it ain't right!

I had heard stories about prostitution being rampant in Havana, but this was my first encounter. I was lucky that it didn't get out of hand and involve the police. Jails in Cuba are not the five-star ones of America; in fact, they have no star rating at all. Besides, no one is supposed to know that I was in Cuba; I would have rotted away in a dark, damp, and dirty jail—with rats, spiders and bats.

El Malecón

I left the flea market—considered taking a cab to my hotel—instead, I hailed a bike-propelled rickshaw. While riding alongside the ocean of the *Malecón*, I suddenly realized that I hadn't walked on the famous promenade—I might as well be looking at another postcard. How could I not take the opportunity to feel the ocean breeze and watch the waves crash onto the rocks—live! I asked Luis, the bike-pedaling tour guy—a handsome black Cuban with blue eyes—to stop short of the hotel and take a picture of me sitting on the *Malecón* wall, with the *Morro* Castle in the background; I told him I would walk to the hotel on my own. Finally, I can be part of this landscape! The driver departed—yelling, "Ask for Luis, when you come back! I'm always here."

While contemplating the crashing waves, a strange man began speaking to me about Jesus. He was poorly dress, but well spoken. A blotch of white cream was on his forehead; perhaps, it was sunblock—except, it wasn't sunny out. The dark clouds were gathering fast and it was beginning to drizzle; but the man kept on talking. I'm sure this guy is a nut and I couldn't wait to get away. He spoke freely about politics—and, that he considered Fidel Castro to be Satan. "Castro is no good," he said. "He wants to destroy Cuba and all the people in it." ..... "Castro doesn't care for anyone, but himself," he shouted. I was getting nervous and started to leave, but he stopped me and spoke some more—putting his arms around my shoulders. I made another attempt to leave and—this time—I really got soaked. He followed me—begging for money; as I crossed the avenue, he kept reaching for my arm. I had a few soaked *pesos* in my pocket, which I gave him in an effort to lose him—which I finally did. Lightning lit up the sky; the rolling roar of thunder made the earth tremble beneath my feet. It was pouring so hard that the raindrops actually hurt on contact. I looked back and saw the crazy man standing in the middle of the street—soaking wet, waving his arms in the air, and shouting, "Bless you, bless you, my friend." I muttered, in disgust, "Friends like him will surely put me in jail!"—and I disappeared into the hotel.

The Stalker

I was soaked from head to toe—as I entered my dark hotel room. The curtains were blowing wildly and everything near the window was wet—due to the recent downpour. I hastily stripped off my wet clothes and, in my nakedness, went to close the window. From the east wing, I noticed a man with binoculars looking in my direction. I instantly became paranoid and quickly closed the curtains. Am I being watched? Is someone spying on me? Why is he looking in my window? My wild imagination started to play tricks on me. Did Castro find out who I was and decided to put a tail on me? Am I being prosecuted for the sins of my rebel family, who fought against Castro? "I know I'm not supposed to be here, Mister Castro," I pleaded, "but I came here for love of country, not for political reasons." "Joey, take hold of yourself," I said to myself—almost slapping my own face. This isn't a spy story or "Rear Wincow." Why should I think of defending myself— I have done nothing—I'm innocent!—I'm innocent, I tell you! "Wow!"— I'm suddenly possessed by Barbara Stanwick!

My nerves were getting the best of me. I went slowly to the window and peeked out through the corner of the drapes; I saw no one at the other window. The man was gone and the drapes were closed. I backed away for a second and quickly looked out again—just in case he was peering out at me, playing the same game. I finally left the window, poured myself a shot of rum, and sat on the bed to calm down. I sat there thinking about the whole episode and started to laugh. "What an idiot I am; it's probably a lonely pervert!"

The Visit

I dashed into the bathroom and took a cold shower; it was getting late and I wanted to visit my cousin, who lived nearby. Changing clothes was easy: I just put on the same shorts that I've been wearing, but with a different tee-shirt, and I was ready to go. (Since I travel light, I didn't bring enough outfits to keep me standing and wondering in front of the closet door—asking, "What shall I wear today?) Truly, all I had hanging in the closet was a suit, 2 tee-shirts, a white dress shirt, and a pair of dress shoes; everything else was still inside the carry-on case. I hadn't even worn the suit jacket; it's been casual attire wherever I go—besides, it's always been too hot for a jacket.

I decided to pack—as to get a head start for tomorrow's trip to Varadero Beach. I left out only the toiletries for the morning shave—those are the last things I put in the suitcase. The tour bus was picking me up at 3:00pm—leaving me with the entire morning to do as I please.

It was 8:00pm and getting late; I had to head out for my cousin's house. I was looking for his address, but I couldn't find it. I looked in my pockets, my suit pants, the shoulder bag—it was nowhere to be found. What am I going to do? Call the telephone operator? That's no good, he doesn't have a phone. The only place left to look was where I had put my travel documents. I rushed to the closet and opened the safe; I was so excited, I kept pressing the wrong codes and the safe wouldn't open. I counted to 10—calmed down—and took my time in punching in the codes—finally, the safe lets me in. I found the address between the pages of my passport—how it got there I'll never know. I probably put it there, just in case I was asked whom I was visiting in Cuba—then, I could conveniently hand them the address. Boy! I was relieved! I grabbed my shoulder bag and dashed to the front desk to ask for directions. The girl at the desk said that, according to the address, it was a short walk from the hotel.

I still felt like a tourist, so I decided to walk the streets and do a little sightseeing; there was about an hour of daylight left and I wanted to mingle with the people. I must have walked two miles—passing small stores that were selling books on *Che Guevara*—and cheap artifacts. There were men sitting on the curb—just people watching—having a beer. By nature, Cubans are friendly and curious towards people. They like to observe the clothes you wear; the color of your eyes; your hair; your teeth; and your shoes. In brief, they're nosy and love to gossip—but, they don't like being the butt of the gossip.

I was now in another part of Havana that I had not seen before; everything here was new to me. The buildings were architecturally beautiful, with arched doorways and stain glass windows—but all were in need of a good paint job. (All of Cuba needs a paint job!) There were many cracks on the cement walls and on most of the sidewalks—requiring repairs. I loved watching the antique cars of the 50's as they drove by; one resembled the car my mother had in

Connecticut. It was aqua, with silver fins—a bit offbeat for a conservative lady to drive.

I remember it—as though it were yesterday—how I learned to drive. I was sixteen years old and a young rebel; no one trusted me enough to teach me to drive. The thought of me behind the wheel didn't cross their minds—not for a minute! The last thing they wanted to see was me behind the wheel of a car—with the wheels turning, that is. My grades in school were not up to par and I was getting into a lot of mischief—all the time. My teachers weren't the greatest and I was bored with school—getting into trouble made my life interesting. But, I was determined to drive; tonight was the night to take control of the car—once and for all.

Learning To Drive

I waited until three in the morning, when everyone was asleep, to make my debut. I sneaked out of my room, still wearing my pajamas, picked up the car keys from the kitchen table, and slowly opened the front door of our third-floor colonial home. Softly, I stepped onto the porch and quietly closed the door behind me. Walking down the stairs, I stepped on a loose board and it made a loud squeak. I froze instantly and my heart skipped several beats—I was afraid that my dad would wake up and shoot me dead, thinking that I was a prowler. I waited in silence for several seconds—listening for the sound of an extra heartbeat behind me. There wasn't any; I only heard my father's earth-trembling snore.

It was safe and I continued with my early morning adventure; I went down the rest of the steps, out the front gate, and climbed into the 1957 Chevy. I didn't want to wake up anyone, so I left the car door open. I studied the panel and rehearsed the pedals: clutch down, shift into 1st gear, give it some gas, slowly release the clutch, ride a little—again: clutch down, shift into 2nd gear, give it lots more gas, slowly release the clutch, ride a little further—one more time, put it in 3rd gear and RIDE, BABY, RIDE!

I slammed the door shut and drove up the block. Coming to a stop sign, I slammed on the brakes and the car went into a skid. I wanted to go farther, so I repeated the same movements and got to the next

39

corner—safely. This time, I put on the brakes—gently. "What a good driver, I am! ..... I'm a natural!" I went once around the block, then around two blocks, then three, four blocks—on the fifth block, I parked the car for a rest and congratulated myself. As I sat there, working up the courage to take the car downtown to show off, a police car—patrolling the neighborhood—cruised by—which scared me from going on. So, I played it safe, gave up the idea of going downtown, parked the car, and went excitedly to bed. And that's how I learned to drive.

Back to The Visit

By now, I was tired of pounding the pavement, looking for my cousin's house—which was nowhere in sight. Two girls passed by and one said to the other, "Wow. That's how I like my men, husky." I don't know if this was a compliment, because I had been dieting to lose weight, but I smiled and said, "Gracias. I'm flattered to know someone out there likes their guy 'husky'."—although, the comment did curb my appetite.

I showed the address to a policeman who was standing at the corner doing absolutely nothing. I was ready to give up the search and walk back to the hotel, but I invested so much time in searching that I was determined to find the address. "It seems your cousin lives far from here," said the policeman. "It's actually too far to walk and it's getting dark; I suggest that you take a cab." I thanked him and angrily hailed a cab.

We drove for about 10 minutes, touring the narrow streets, which were filled with huge potholes. People were hanging out from windows, talking with friends; kids were playing in the dark streets, while others sat by their doorsteps—just trying to keep cool. Some men sat in groups and mingled together on street corners—drinking cheap beer. Screaming mothers called after their children to come into the house, with kids yelling back—begging for more time to play. Not a very respectable and quiet neighborhood, but very colorful and earthy.

The driver made a left turn and drove slowly on a bumpy cobblestone street—stopping in the middle of the block. "This is it," he said. It was dark on the one-way street and I cautiously looked out the window; before getting out, I asked the driver to wait for me—so I wouldn't be stranded if no one was home. (It can be extremely dangerous for a stranger alone in this part of town.) The driver parked a few doors away—half on and half off the sidewalk—to make room for other cars to pass; then, he shut the headlights off and it really got dark. The streetlights went off at that instant—as they do every night, for a few hours—to save energy. Only the dim glow of burning candles in the homes lit the street. I stepped out of the cab and walked past a window, where a pretty young girl with blonde hair was speaking with a man standing on the sidewalk. "Romeo and Juliet—through bars—and without a balcony." was my thought. Her eyes followed me when I passed the window and—in anticipation of my visit—she opened the door before I had a chance to knock. "Good evening," she said. "How can I help you?" "Well. My name is *José Infante* and I'm from New York City. The family calls me *Papi* and I'm looking for my cousin, Ramón." Upon hearing these words, she threw her arms around me—tears came to her eyes. "I'm your cousin too; your cousin, Ramón, is my adopted father!" I was emotionally charged—after being greeted so warmly by a family member that I had never met. Excited and speaking a mile a minute, she told me that Ramón has been hospitalized for the last two weeks. I suggested that we go to the hospital right away, because this was the only time that I could see him. She grabbed some cookies and we went hurriedly to the waiting cab. "Close my door," she screamed at her friend—who was waiting by the window. "I'm going to the hospital." She gave the driver the address and asked him to fly—we haven't much time; it was now 9:45pm and the hospital doors close at 10:00pm.

On the way to the hospital, we shared many things. She asked many questions, one after another, without taking a breath—at the same time, she ate a cookie She gave me a cookie, which I practically swallowed whole. I was hungry, but I didn't want to take her food. The cookies reminded me of my father's cookies. I tell her about my unsuccessful quest to find a cookie similar to the one Papá used to bake and she laughed. (Many cookies look alike, but they don't taste like Papá's.)

At Dracula's Castle (The Hospital)

Just ahead stood the imposing hospital; but before we got out of the cab, I asked the driver to pick me up in an hour—to take me back to my hotel. He agreed. Niurka—as she is called—was staying overnight at the hospital to look after her dad.

We stood by the curbside, gazing up at the great building; it was dark and eerie. The dimly-lit windows—from lack of power—gave a mysterious and menacing sensation. The surrounding neighborhood was just as creepy; the houses looked abandoned, with tall, unkept grass growing wildly. I felt as if I was approaching Dracula's castle.

As we climbed the cracked cement stairs, my cousin assured me that this was the finest hospital in the area. She said that the doctors and care facility were the best; and it was the only place in town to get a decent meal. It was dark and musty inside—and it smelled of rubbing alcohol. The marble floors had no shine and the bare walls were peeling. I supposed that patient care was more important than the upkeep of the structure—or the decor. The elevator wasn't running, so we used the stairs to get to the second floor. I could hear patients moaning from pain, others screaming in agony—as we passed the open rooms. Some walked in the hallways, holding onto the walls—wearing white, open-back hospital robes, exposing their backsides; some just stood around with a blank, far-away look in their eyes; others, on crutches, made their way to the bathroom—hoping that they would get there in time. They all seemed like zombies lurking in the dark shadows of the halls. The pungent odor of sickness—and of strong medications—filtered out to the halls. I felt as I if I was in a leper colony—and I couldn't wait to get out. (I have come all this way; I must see it through.)

Ten minutes passed and no nurse in sight. Arriving at Ramón's room, my cousin stopped me and said, "Wait out here while I tell my father that I've got a surprise for him." I asked myself, "What surprise? The man doesn't know me from Adam; how can he be surprised?" Just the same, I stood outside the room and waited for him to come out to be surprised.

Moments later, a handsome older man with thick gray hair came to the door and gave me a puzzled look. I stood there with a smile, waiting for him to be 'surprised.' "You look familiar," said a soft, crackly voice. "But I don't know you; who are you?" "I'm your cousin, *José Infante*, from New York," I told him, loudly. He smiled and greeted me cheerfully—with a big smile. I was certain that he didn't know who I was, but I entered his room—in which, there were two army-barrack style beds, a rocking chair, and an old recliner (where his room companion sat half asleep or drugged), and a broken stool. (And this is the best hospital!) We talked for a long time, while his daughter made a pot of black Cuban coffee. Ramón worked up the courage to confront me and finally asked—in a stronger voice, "Now, who are you? I'm confused. I'm talking to you as if I know you and I still don't know who you are." "Who are you?" he asked again. I realized that he was getting upset, so I explained slowly, "I'm the son of *María Castellanos* from *Banes;* my family calls me *Papi.* You haven't seen me in over half a century. You used to baby-sit me." Upon hearing my mother's name, he got up from the rocking chair, with tears in his eyes, and hugged me tightly—repeating my name. *Papi, Papi*—he kept on repeating my name. "Is it really you?" Tears flooded my eyes; I was overwhelmed with emotion—and his daughter tearfully came to his side to calm him down. "Dad, please sit down; it's no good for you to get too excited. It's OK, it's OK, please relax. Remember your blood pressure. *Papi,* come. Help me sit him down." We sat Ramón in the rocker and gave him a glass of water to calm him down; I sat on the stool next to him, holding his shaking, cold hand—while his daughter served the coffee.

Ramón and I gossiped about everyone in the family. He asked about Mamá and Papá, my sisters—Cachita, Misael, Melba—and my brother, Rodolfo. I told him that Rodolfo got Alzheimer's at the age of 74 and went to a nursing home in Miami, Florida; but he has since died. Rodolfo was an abusive husband and father and I truly believe that he's now paying for his sins. I'm sorry to say that I have no attachments to him, but I don't remember him as a part of my life—nor as a loving and caring brotherly figure. However, I do remember how nasty and destructive he was. Later on, Rodolfo realized the damage that he had caused me, but never apologized; that was beneath his arrogant manhood. He begged me to take care of his son, if he should die before his child became an adult, but it was too late. Rodolfo ruined many lives—especially the lives of his own family. I forgave him, but I didn't forget. Then again, during his illness, he didn't know which end was up, so I guess he's not receiving much of a punishment; he probably doesn't know that he's suffering—or even dead.

Ramón said that my sister, Cachita, was one of the most talented women from the Southern part of Cuba; At 12, Cachita was singing opera regularly on CMQ, the national radio station—against my father's will. Cachita became a celebrity reminiscent of Jane Powell and Deanna Durbin—when they were all young singers. Everybody called Cachita "Kary" and Ramón remembers her as strikingly beautiful and blessed with long, luxurious, black wavy hair, and an eighteen inch waistline. Wherever Kary walked, eyes followed. In those days, women of the theater were not accepted by proper society. Papá didn't approve of any of his children becoming entertainers; oddly enough, we all became involved in the theater—with the exception of Rodolfo, who had no talent worth developing. Now, I'm the only one who—from time to time—performs in a Cabaret. I love entertaining, but I wouldn't consider leaving my day job. Every so often, I work up an act, gather several musicians, invite my friends to a club, and we all have a great evening together. Everyone else in the family is retired, married, very religious, or busy raising children. To each their own—I'm still flying high and free.

Melba, my 'cute as a button' other sister, won a Shirley Temple lookalike contest—as a child; later, as a teenager, Melba received numerous prizes for baton twirling, and she led many grand parades. Melba was a tomboy, who would climb trees and eat fruits—while they were still on the branch—way up high. Melba was my protector; no harm ever came to me, as long as she was around. But no one protected me from Melba—when I'd stick my tongue out at her. Melba would run after me, beat me gently, and—then—tickle the hell out of me. I loved getting Melba mad—I still do!

My third sister, Misael, is a widow and lives in Connecticut—helping to raise her grandchildren. I remember Misael as having a stunning soprano voice and singing in the church choir, which all my sisters did. Misael was fine singing with others; alone, she was a nervous wreck. Tired of fighting her demons, Misael settled down and married Richard, a wonderful guy. Richard was an architect and he built Misael a palatial home. Richard cherished Misael and, together, they made two beautiful children; he will not be forgotten. I'm now blessed with gorgeous nieces and handsome nephews, with children of their own. I'm proud to say that I'm a great granduncle and I'm loved very much by "my children"—since I have none of my own.

Time passed quickly on this trip down memory lane. Ramón and I needed more than one day to catch up on all the years that have slipped through—perhaps, next year. The other patient in the room sat in his recliner, listening expressionless to our stories—without uttering a single word. He was in a catatonic state—or looked like he was. It was a full hour before we saw the first health professional, who came to tell me that my cab was waiting. Ramón and his roommate could have been kidnapped or killed and the hospital personnel wouldn't have detected ANYTHING—and this is the best that Havana has to offer.

I wished that I could have stayed longer—to share more family stories; but time was not on my side. We said our farewell and I handed my cousin an envelope containing a gift of money, which was on behalf of his sister, Ofelia, her daughter, Daisy, and me. Ramón walked me out to the steps and hugged and kissed me; he asked me to come back real soon, before he dies, because we have so much to talk about. I didn't think that I would cry in the company of a man that I hardly knew; yet, because he is family and he knew so much about my family, it all mattered.

Ramón's daughter accompanied me to the waiting cab and gently kissed my forehead. She thanked me for my inspiring and welcomed visit. Before I entered the cab, I urged her to go inside—I wanted to see her safe—before departing.

It was dark and humid outside; it felt like rain was on the way. I opened the car door—as a roll of thunder and a crack of lightning lit up the sky. This time, I felt like I was entering.....Dracula's horse-driven carriage.

By now, the cab driver was almost a family member. He took me into his confidence and shared his views on the political virus that's infesting this country that he loves so much. I could feel his blood pressure rising, as he sped through the narrow streets. I told him to stay calm and slow down; I didn't want him to get into an accident. Hoping to restore him to his senses, I said to him, "I've heard rumors that before his term in office ends, President Clinton is going to terminate the embargo; Clinton wants to be perceived throughout history as the president who re-establishes diplomatic relations with Cuba." The cab driver started to relax and listened. "I assure you that Cuba will once again be the democratic country it once was; tourists will again flock to its shores and enjoy its Latin hospitality." Looking at me through the rearview mirror, he excitedly exclaimed, "from your mouth to God's ears, my friend; I truly hope so; I truly hope so!"

Coppelia's

The rain clouds disappeared and it became a beautiful evening. The sky was full of twinkling stars—which would have tantalized Galileo. It was too early to go to sleep; besides, I had already packed for my trip to Varadero Beach. I was getting hungry and I wanted a late supper. I didn't want to eat at the hotel, so I opt for a neighborhood restaurant. I asked the driver to drop me off on the corner, near the hotel, so that I can take a last walk on the city's busy streets. I stood in front of many restaurants, reading the menus,; nothing appealed to me. I was craving a typical Cuban dish, but all they were serving was ham and cheese sandwiches. I remembered now that I had a Cuban sandwich back in my room, from last night's snack, which I didn't finish. I like to keep food handy, for when I get hungry in the middle of the night; especially in a hotel, where it's difficult to get room service late at night. I decided to go to *Coppelia's*—for Havana's finest ice cream. *Coppelia* is nestled in a block-size park, four blocks from the *Hotel Nacional.* The park is a rain forest in the middle of Havana. Situated in the center, looking like a UFO, surrounded by tropical foliage, stands the ice cream parlor. Everyone goes there for their sugar fix— me included. This ice cream has no rival in Cuba; it's pure heaven.

The Prostitute

I'm a vanilla type of guy, but don't let that fool you; there's still a lot of flavor left in me! I was sitting under a tree that was softly lit green by a park lamp—indulging in four scoops of incredibly delicious vanilla ice cream, minding my own business. At this moment, the world did not exist; just me and my ice cream. A lovely girl in a purple wig sat in the seat next to me; she didn't say a word, she just sat. She crossed her legs to attract my attention.....and sat some more in silence. I continued ignoring her, not bothering to look up from my dish of ice cream; there was more silence and I kept eating. I sensed her strong presence gazing at me—I chose to keep ignoring her. I was totally involved with the dessert, but I watched her from the corner of my eye. Not a word was spoken—she squirmed and crossed her legs again and again, trying to attract my attention. My curiosity was aroused, but I wanted to sit and savor my dessert—that is, before it melted from the heat of this night (in more ways than one). Without looking up, I broke the silence and asked, "Are you hungry?" She contemplated the thought and sweetly answered, "No." "Would you like some ice cream?" "Not right now; perhaps later; yes?" she said. "Later, I won't be here; you'll have to decide now." I waited for her response, as I licked the last drop of cream from the spoon—when another girl with a green wig walked by, snapped her finger, and my new friend left—smiling. "Bye, thanks for the offer; see you around," she said, and they both disappeared into the dark foliage. I had no more ice cream—and never made eye contact with either of them. I laughingly searched for the invasion of party wigs, but there was none. They had all gone—disappeared—poof! Almost disappointed, I went back to the spaceship and got more ice cream; then, headed home to prepare for tomorrow's ride.

Peeping Into Windows

I zig-zagged the four blocks back to the hotel. I went up one street for two blocks, down the other street for another two blocks, and so on—admiring the architecture. I'm a self-proclaimed decorating aficionado; I've always been curious about how people adorn their homes. I love to peep into windows and see what the masses hang on their walls—and, their paintings: are they of landscapes, animals, portraits of family members, or persons from the middle ages—with no relation to them whatsoever? Chandeliers or light fixtures? Are the walls adorned with paint or paper? Are the floors, natural wood, carpet, or tile? What color and style are the furnishings, and from what are they made—glass, wood, plastic—or are they antiques? Are there photographs of children and loved ones on furniture tops for display? (You can tell a lot about a family by what they keep in their homes.) All these thoughts ran through my mind, as I passed open, unobstructed windows—inviting me to look in.

Growing up in Cuba and the USA, I have seen my homes get bigger and the furniture get better. In Cuba, I remember a small house with an eat-in kitchen—which had a tree growing through the roof. My sisters, Melba and Misael, shared a bedroom; I slept in my parent's room. A small living room completed the home. The second was larger by two additional rooms and the third was a dirt floor basement—as we, waited for departure to America. My sister, Cachita, was already married when I was born—and had her own mansion.

In America, my first home was on a third floor walk-up—on the corner of State Street and Park Avenue—in Bridgeport, Connecticut. There was a Catholic Church facing the apartment on the opposite side of the street—in which bells played throughout the day. I used to love to listen to the bells play a song—every hour on the hour—and then—gong the time. The bells only chimed once on the half-hour. I couldn't sleep for the first two months in this new and strange country. Like Quasimodo, I finally adjusted to the ringing bells and didn't hear them anymore—at least, not at night. To this day, the chimes of church bells take me back to a wonderful new beginning in America.

In America

It's October 1947 and I don't start school until the following year. The family is trying to acclimate to the cool weather, the new people, and our neighborhood. I spend a lot of time looking out the window and eating red, delicious apples. Golden-red-brown leaves have fallen off the trees by mid-November and we celebrated our first Thanksgiving with new friends and neighbors; each cooked their favorite dish to share. There was so much food, that we didn't know where to begin. I ate too much and got sick—but I remember well the pumpkin pie with vanilla ice cream. I'll never forget how we all thought the world was coming to an end—when we saw the first snowfall of the season. It was the middle of December and the frozen water came down in buckets. Some nights were so cold that we slept with our coats on underneath the blankets. It snowed for five days straight and everything was covered with white flakes of ice. I had a strange disease called the "flu" and I couldn't go out to play—so I would put my hands out the window to catch the snow, which melted instantly from the heat of my hands. "Close the window, you're going to catch pneumonia," Mamá would scream. I'd close the window and the glass would fog up—giving me an opportunity to practice my art by drawing funny faces on it; then, I would sign my new American name, "JOSEPH." When the window cleared, the funny faces and my name would still be smudged on the glass; I'd wipe the glass down with a cloth and, when nobody was looking, start drawing again. We celebrated our first "White Christmas."

Back to Window Peeping

My window peeping journey ended, as I passed the notorious *Hotel Capri.* It was 10:00pm and I was just in time to see another world famous floor show. I was so excited, I ran for a whole block—practically killing myself, while crossing the street. I quickly climbed the stairs to the lobby, hoping that there will be space left for me in the Cabaret. I was out of breath; but, upon entering the hotel, I was totally unimpressed. It was plain and unattractive—not at all what I had pictured from the fabulous stories that I've been told. The *Hotel Capri* is now rundown and badly maintained—what a letdown! For a moment, I forgot why I came; but I recovered quickly—standing in an empty lobby. I wondered where the people were. "They must all be in the Cabaret," were my thoughts. I decided to investigate and I went to the showroom. I peered through the closed doors and saw the tables and chairs were all stacked up and off the floor. Obviously, there wasn't going to be any show tonight! There were just two men cleaning the room and blasting salsa music from a radio. They were so engrossed in their happiness that one of them started dancing with a broom, while the other man held his mop upside down—making it look like a girl—with long, stringy, blonde, dirty hair. They danced happily with their brooms—in tempo with the music. If they practiced, they might have a good act and never have to scrub floors again. (It's funny what men do when they're not being watched; we're all just children at heart!)

The hotel host tapped me on the shoulder and told me that there was no shows on Monday. "Oh," I said, with a gleaming smile in my eyes. "I did see the show and it was great! When I come back next year, I'll see the other show; but I don't think it'll be half as good as the one I've just seen." I thanked the man, gave him a wink, and walked out. I'm sure I left him puzzled, because I saw him scratching his head.

This being my last night in Havana, I didn't want to go to sleep. Instead, I went to the garden and sat on a lounge chair, which overlooked the dark ocean. I could see every star in the heavens—sparkling like precious diamonds. There was a warm, hypnotic breeze making its way through my hair. The glow of the full moon made the breaking waves appear white with shimmering silver foam. I closed my eyes and fell into a deep sleep—caressed by drops of water from a passing cloud. I gazed around the garden, in awe of the iridescent fireflies shining among the flowers—and circling my head. I was floating—I was playing among the stars—it was pure fantasy.

I remembered that I still had half a Cuban sandwich waiting to be eaten; I should be hungry—supper was just a dish of ice cream. I headed for the elevator and pressed the button—thinking that the harder I pressed, the quicker it would come. I had to take control of myself: "it's only a machine, Joe, and it'll do whatever it's programmed to do." That's what I kept telling myself; but this elevator was taking its time getting to the lobby—just to annoy me. The door opened and I dashed in as fast as I could and pressed the fourth floor button, while simultaneously pressing the "close door" button—which actually cancelled each other out, confusing the lift. I didn't want anyone else in the elevator interrupting this ride towards my waiting sandwich. My stomach was growling terribly and I wished that the elevator would go faster than a speeding bullet—which, of course, it didn't. "It's only a machine...it's only a machine...it's only a machine." That's what I kept repeating, until I was back in my room—nibbling my Cuban sandwich and drinking a *Cuba Libre* chaser. *Cuba Libres* are very refreshing, but a couple of these will do you for the night. This was the best rum that I had ever had and it was a shame to mix it with anything—other than ice.

I was sitting by the window, with drink in hand, recalling today's adventures; this evoked a feeling of great sadness. It was my last night in Havana and I was taking a long, enduring look at the city that was four stories below. The panoramic view of the skyscrapers, the romantic *Malecón* Promenade, the vast night sky with the moon and stars hovering over an indigo-blue sea, wave after wave reflecting the light as far as the eye can see—I wanted this view embedded in my memory—forever. The *Cuba Libres* were taking effect and my lids were getting heavy; I wanted to close my eyes. The bed was beckoning, more than the shower that I should take. I undressed and noticed that the air conditioning was not on. The maid had turned it off, but left a window open, which kept the room comfortably cool. There was a light ocean breeze blowing, which made the heat bearable; but weather in the tropics changes quickly and now it was beginning to do just that—and the humidity was making it hot. I wasn't about to sleep in this heat—which suddenly overcame me. I closed the window, turned on the air, and considered the people trying to sleep in this clammy, balmy August heat—without air-conditioning. How uncomfortable! "Oh"—"But they must be used to it." With that comforting thought, I fell fast asleep—in seconds. The shower can wait until morning...ZZZZZZZZZZZZ.

El Morro Castle

My rooster alarm watch was crowing louder than I ever heard it crow before; I hurriedly struggled to shut the alarm off—before the man next door started banging on the wall again—screaming, yelling, and threatening to kill my bird. There was a hard knock on the door and I was afraid my neighbor was getting aggressive—so I wrapped myself up with a sheet and grabbed the bottle of rum for protection. I was ready for this guy, but what a pity if I had to waste the rum on his head. Expecting a confrontation, I defiantly marched to the door—head high, while my heart was frantically beating. I hastily opened the door—holding the bottle behind me, ready to strike. "*Buenos días, señor,*" said a lovely, gentle voice. "Would you like your room cleaned now?" My heart stopped pounding and an embarrassing feeling came over me; I stood there—looking like the Statue of Liberty. I felt terribly stupid—not to mention cowardly—but I was relieved that it was only this fragile little girl, all five feet tall and skinny like a rail confronting me—not the two hundred and fifty pound German wrestler. "Not now, *señorita*...I'm checking out soon and I have to first pack and clean up...then, the room is yours." She put on a sweet smile and wished me a safe trip.

I drew the curtains back and was almost blinded by the bright morning star. The sky was the baby blue of a Tiffany box. Before the 2:00pm bus heading to Varadero picks me up, there was one more sight in Havana for me to see. (Anyway, it doesn't take more than ten minutes to pack everything; I've learned to travel extremely light.) I showered off the dust from yesterday—and I was feeling rambunctious and ready to go.

Check out was a breeze. They stored my carry-on luggage inside a locked room in the lobby and told me that I had three hours until departure. (There's a lot that you can do in Havana in that amount of time—most places of interest are never too far away.) No time to waste—so I ran out and hailed a cab. "*El Morro, por favor.*" I had three hours to play and I wanted to make the most of them!

I've spent so many years looking at photographs of the famous fortress of *El Morro*—and its lighthouse—that it's hard to believe that I was finally stepping foot inside this fortress. I knew that I'd pass through every room and touch every wall of this monument—Cuba's #1 landmark. I've never seen pictures of the interior, so that will be new. I thought that a boat ride was the only means of transportation to the lighthouse, but it can also be easily reached by car. After a 15-minute panoramic drive along the *Malecón*, we arrived at the parking lot adjacent to *El Morro*. I asked the driver to take a *siesta* and wait for me, while I made my visit. I promised to generously pay him for his time. "You're the boss," he said. "My day is at your disposal; I'll wait for you under the shade of the banana tree."

I grabbed my camera and made my way to the top of the small hill. Reaching the top, I faced the back of the lighthouse, the vast open sea was to the right of me, and an impressive view of Havana harbor was to the left. I was finally here—inside the picture postcard—and it only took half a century to reach. I stood up there for a long time, contemplating the view and making sure that I could replay it in my mind—when I got back home. The fortress was desolate at 10:00am; I got my wish—to be the first one to set foot on the big rock on this—my lucky day—August 24th. I stamped my feet on the rock—to confirm that I was actually standing there. I still had a feeling of disbelief...am I really here?

On the first landing, above the waterless moat (which was now covered with grass), were several vendors setting up shop: dolls dressed up in traditional Cuban costumes; wood-carved African figurines; decorative seashells; funny faces made out of coconut shells; jewelry fashioned from black coral; and musical instruments—such as maracas, miniature guitars, and bongo drums; postcards and books on Cuban history and *El Morro*—all were on sale. The hot items were tee-shirts and picture books of *El Che*. Salsa music was everywhere. On exhibition—along the trail leading to a walk-bridge which crossed over to the entrance of the fortress—were plaques describing Cuba's great moments in history. I read each one—wondering if any of my ancestors took part in the making of Cuban history.

El Morro's full title is "the Castle of the Three Holy Kings." This fortress was built from blocks excavated from the coastal reefs of Cuba; it took 40 years to complete the massive structure. There are still several cannons, pointing in symbolic defiance towards the US—guarding against an invasion. On the lower level is the "Battery of the Twelve Apostles," where twelve cannons were on exhibition; each one named after an apostle. Traditionally, these guns were fired at 9:00pm during colonial times—to announce the closing of the city's gates; today, guards in Spanish colonial uniforms reenact the firing of the cannons—with blanks.

I passed through these imposing, arched, black iron gates and bought a ticket to a castle adventure. In the front room was a boutique, with clothing for both men and women. Hand-embroidered cotton dresses and straw handbags for the women; fancy *Guallavera* shirts for the men. On the other side were displayed cannons, shields, guns, spears, iron balls, and all kinds of weapons used for killing. I strolled out to the courtyard, and was confronted by a maze of passageways—all leading in different directions: some went up; some went down; with lots of stairs to climb. There were many open rooms, with arched entrances, that were used for different purposes: there was the stock room; the dining room; the weapons room; and, the meeting and recreation room. At the far left of the courtyard was a small opening, with a narrow staircase leading to the jail cells—where acts of torturous cruelty were perpetuated. I keep scraping the top of my head on the low ceilings, especially when ascending the stairs; people in those days were obviously smaller. I had expected unbearable heat, but it

53

was rather cool inside the three-foot, thick-walled rooms. Further inside, there was an exhibit of early grass housing or huts, which depicted how the Taíno and the Siboney Indians lived during Pre-Colombian Cuban times. I studied the old maps that hung on the wall, which showed the route that Christopher Columbus took to cross the Atlantic Ocean—eventually leading to the colonization of the Americas; this was an education in itself. I examined the artifacts, as if I were seeing them for the very first time—which I was. In New York City, the Museum of Natural History is only a five-minute walk from my apartment; I visit often. I'm no stranger to history, but—since this is part of my heritage and I'm here now—I was especially interested in these particular artifacts.

There were three rooms joined by arched doorways, but all were empty. The architects in those days must have preferred to build arches, because arches were everywhere: arches for windows, for doors, for buildings; narrow ones, fat ones, tall ones, two-story and three-story high ones. I kept searching for a normal door, but I didn't find one. In reality, doors were only large holes in the wall, which united two separate rooms. Presently, *El Morro* is undergoing major renovations—to make it more interesting and educational for tourists not familiar with Cuban history.

Down I went the narrow stairwell, scraping my head again—this time, leaving some hair behind on the ceiling. I had to get to the lighthouse before it got too late.

I felt like a child again—skipping down the cobblestone road towards the long, anticipated hike to the top of the lighthouse; and, after walking through a few narrow paths and climbing up a few stairs, I was faced with the open door that began the winding ascension. Before I entered, I stood there, slowly scanning upwards towards the top. I was mesmerized; at the same time, I felt anger and hatred towards Castro—for taking away my right to visit this place—for so many years.

This early in the day, I was the only person here and I took full advantage of the occasion. I laid on the pavement to stare up at the lighthouse. It appeared to be moving, as the clouds passed from behind—leaving a hypnotic effect. I was lying on the warm, damp ground—with my eyes closed, feeling totally relax (to the point of falling asleep)—when I heard a man shouting, "Mister, are you all right? Hey, you down there, are you OK?" I opened my eyes and looked up, but I couldn't see anybody. The top of the lighthouse was right in front of the sun and there was a blinding reflection. I could hear the man shouting—more clearly, now. For an instance, I imagined I was having a heavenly experience; but I quickly regained my senses and yelled back, "Yes, I'm OK, thank you." I took a final look at this structure, which has been guiding ships since 1845. It's light can be clearly seen as far as fifty miles out to sea; some people say that on a clear day, from the top of the lighthouse, you can see the lights glowing in Key West.

I began the climb to the top of the lighthouse by way of a narrow, spiral staircase—stopping at every two landings to catch my breath. I suppose I'm a bit out of shape; but so is half the world's population. I started to count the steps on the way up, but I lost count by the fourth landing—due to the distraction of the views from the windows. With my hotel room key, I discreetly carved my name on one of the window shutters. Although the scratching sound of the key scraping the hard wood could be heard throughout the lighthouse, I boldly finish etching my signature. I had forgotten where I was for a moment and quickly got on my way—leaving the mischievousness behind. I assume the jail term for defacing government property in Castro's world is LIFE IMPRISONMENT; I don't know...or care—I just wanted to leave my mark on the lighthouse. On my next visit, I'll search for my signature, inscribed on the window shutter; for now, I've become part of the history of the lighthouse. I was out of breath when I got to the top, reaching for the extended hand of the man—who, earlier, was shouting at me. We greeted each another and he apologized for previously startling me. He said that he was concerned that something had happened to me. I explained to him that I had been contemplating the view from the ground up. "I thought you fainted or something...you know...heat stroke," he says. "I looked down and there you were...lying on the ground...No one has ever done that before." I thanked him for his concern and we both laughed. The tall, thin, handsome man was obviously of Spanish descent; he had gentle blue eyes, was about 65-years old, and his face was strong, weathered, and sun-tanned—which made him look older than he was. He was the fourth generation of lighthouse keepers and countless times during his watch, he had witnessed tropical storms and hurricanes carrying wild, savage, turbulent winds that sent twenty-five foot walls of angry, merciless sea water—crashing with unforgiving force into his beloved lighthouse. His days as a lighthouse keeper were sadly coming to an end. He loved every minute of the day—watching the sun streak across the sky and feeding the sea gulls that circled around his nest built of bricks and concrete. He enjoyed welcoming visitors from all over the world; it made him feel important. Yet, he was also quite content to hand this wonderful and terrifying excitement over to his heir apparent—upon retirement.

We step outside his nest for a panoramic view of Havana harbor and the great open sea. The breeze was gentle and warm—as I faced the direction of America...America!...What a wonderful word—It rings high when I say it aloud. America means liberty and freedom; but I can't help thinking how close we are, yet so far apart. I'm standing a mere ninety miles from Key West; but it feels like I'm on the other side of the world. My people are so close to freedom; yet, it is so hard to obtain. Perhaps, the Cuban people are being punished for their expression of greed. In the olden days, some had little, while others had much more. At least, we owned ourselves and we made due with what little we had. We lived happily: raising our children and rejoicing in new births; celebrating birthdays and holidays; worshipping the God of our choosing; freely mourning our dead and tending to our everyday chores. Those were not easy times, but we were free. Today, everyone belongs to the State. There is access to free schooling and hospital care, and everyone is considered equal—but everyone has lost their freedom. We have become beggars—dependent on our families, who live outside of Cuba, for food and medical supplies and the Grand Dollar. We cannot make due with what the government provides. "We are a starving and dying nation; we have lost our dignity. "My Cuban people are a proud race and, sometimes, a pretentious one," said the lighthouse keeper. "Could this be our punishment?"

The Escape

The telephone rang and the lighthouse keeper, who remains nameless, went to answer it—leaving me alone to survey the view. I can see the Capitol Building, the *Prado* Promenade, and many of the monuments and hotels that line the *Malecón* Wall. It looked like a miniature toy-city, laid out in front of me, so that I can move the buildings around like a game of checkers. Several coast guard ships patrolling the coast interrupted this peaceful scene. Again, I'm forced back into reality and the realization that dreaming in Cuba is strictly forbidden. Daydreaming, in particular, is a sure way towards disaster and distraction. After spending thirty minutes of nostalgia, perched on the rim of the lighthouse, it was time to get back to the mainland. I took a last look at the vista and, upon approaching the exit, I overheard two men speaking low. "I think Juan Miguel is going to escape tonight, at midnight; he'll make his getaway during the changing of the coast guard. He's got a small, old wooden boat, with a rigged-up motor that boasts a rusty propeller, which a friend who works at the Hemingway Marina gave him. He's taking his wife, his 10-year old daughter, and his widowed mother-in-law. His brother chickened out and is staying behind with his 80-year old mother." "Shush, I hear someone coming up the stairs," whispers the lighthouse keeper. "Here, make believe you're talking on the telephone." Then, I hear the fast shuffling of feet and I can't believe that I'm becoming a part of someone's secret plan to escape. I'm trembling and my blood pressure is steadily climbing— from thinking of the years that I will spend in a rotten Cuban dungeon, if I get caught in the company of these conspiring men. How am I going to make my exit? I'm getting dramatic now and I look for a rope hanging from the side of the lighthouse to climb down. There is no rope or emergency escape ladder attached anywhere. I can't believe this is happening! If only I had my cell-phone; but what good is a cell-phone so far away from home—no one will hear me. I'm covering my mouth to keep from saying something crazy; my heart is beating so hard that I swear everyone can hear its pounding. "Good afternoon, ladies. Welcome to *El Morro*. I suppose that you're both exhausted from the hike up the stairs. Would you like some water?" The lighthouse keeper is speaking in a sigh-of-relief type of tone. "*Sí, por favor, usted es muy amable*," said one woman, who may be an American Spanish teacher with a heavy Southern accent. It was the perfect moment for my escape. I entered the room and both men look at me in shock—like they've seen a ghost; then, they look at each other and then back at me, not knowing what to do. I greeted the women and told them that I was also an American on vacation. I turned to the men and said quickly, "Don't worry, I didn't hear a thing. I come from a free

country called America and I wish you all the luck in the world. *Adiós,
amigos.* May God be with you." The men, reluctantly, said goodbye,
while the women screech "See y'all later, honey; y'all have a good time
now, you hear." I ran down the steps so fast that the stairs were a blur.
(I thought I would never get down from the perch.)

I was back on solid ground—once again. I wiped the sweat from my
face, raised my head to the sky, and thanked God for allowing me to
escape. As much as I enjoyed the visit, that's just how fast I wanted to
get away. I hasten my footsteps, looking back at the lighthouse.
Tripping on the cobblestones, I waved at the two men, who were
watching me from the top, and they waved back—hesitantly.

"I'm out of here! I'm out of here!" I kept telling myself, as I quicken my
pace. If I make it safely back to the taxi, I'll be good, I promise, I'll
redeem myself! I'll even get religious! I ran through the stone corridors,
as if something evil was chasing me. Fear! My own fear was chasing
me. I know there's nothing to fear but fear itself, and I was doing a
damn good job of it. Tourists! I see people up ahead...I'm saved!

Leaving the fortress behind, I am now among the vendors and surrounded by tourists. I made my way through the large crowd, searching for my waiting cab. A car pulled up and I heard the words, "Get in."
I looked inside the car and saw my driver; only now, he was in a different car. More espionage!—I thought. He explained that he had got-
ten a flat on the other car, which doesn't have a spare, but that he did
have a spare car. Cubans! I'll never figure them out. They have a
spare car, but no spare tires.

I spent one and a-half exciting hours at the lighthouse and I have
another hour to sightsee—before returning to the hotel. I asked the
driver to just wander around and show me some sights. We rode
along 5th Avenue, viewing the ex-homes of the rich and famous, now
occupied by heads-of-state. The houses showed signs of a grand
past.

Ahead, soldiers carrying machine guns lined up on both sides of the
road. We were approaching one of the many homes owned or taken
over by Fidel Castro. The road was closed to all traffic and we were
stopped at gun point and told to turn around and leave the area. I
hoped to catch a glimpse of the "Main Man," but I was not about to
argue with seven machine guns pointing in our direction—not to mention the bazookas. We slowly turned the car around—without making

58

any sudden moves that might provoke or excite the guards—and headed down 5th Avenue towards *El Malecón*. I had enough life threatening moments for today, so I decided to calmly abandon the tour and return to the hotel in one piece.

I deserve to spend some quiet, relaxing time at the beach and just chill out. The driver gave me his home address and telephone number, so that I can call him on my return trip to Cuba. He promised a Cuban feast of baked pig cooked on an open pit—with rice & beans, yucca, plantains, and plenty of garlic sauce; everything prepared with *Guajiro-style* trimmings and topped off with plenty of *mojitos*. My mouth waters every time I think about this.

Varadero Beach

I retrieved my suitcase from the porter and waited outside the hotel for the bus that was going to take me to "paradise." It was two in the afternoon and I should have known that the bus was not going to be on time. This is Cuba, a Caribbean island; everyone is on *mañana-time*. I waited for one very hot, humid hour—when the bus finally showed. In the meantime, I could have drowned myself in a few daiquiris and mellowed out from my unforgettable adventures.

The bus was already half full and I couldn't wait to get on board so that I could enjoy the air conditioning. The driver went inside the Hotel and escorted 15 other guests, who were also going to Varadero Beach. I made sure that I was the first on board to get a window seat, so that I can film the countryside. Besides, I did sweat it out waiting for over an hour in the heat. My one and only suitcase was stored under the bus and I took the window seat—on the right side of the bus, facing inland. To the left side of the bus would be the ocean, but I wanted to see the countryside; I'll get to see enough of that sparkling blue sea—when I reach my destination. The air conditioning was heavenly; it was almost cold. The motor coach was also surprisingly, and unexpectedly, comfortable; plus, very modern. The driver closed the doors and pulled away; I suddenly remembered that I had left the best bottle of rum I have ever tasted inside the mini bar. The bottle is a quarter full, but it's a quarter of rum that I would have enjoyed—who knows when I'll have the pleasure of his company again?

"Welcome aboard the Cubanacan tour bus—destination, Varadero Beach. My name is Miguel and I'll be your driver for the day. We'll make a few stops along the way to pick up other passengers; the bus number is 24 and I advise you to write it down—in case of lost articles. Thank you and have a pleasant trip."

We pull out of the palm tree-lined driveway and I looked back to wave good-bye to the hotel that has regally hosted my stay in Havana. I get a last look at the city—as the bus stops at several hotels to pick up passengers. Under my breath, I mumble quietly, sadly: "Cuba, you haven't seen the last of me yet."

There's a sense of the surreal—as we head south along the coast-line. On the outskirts of the city, we pass what I would consider major graffiti. Buildings are covered with anti-American slogans. *Cuba sí! Yankee no!* is written under the faces of Castro and "*El Che.*" In the 60's they chanted this infamous slogan. Today, I tried not to dwell on this negativity, because it makes me angry every time I read one of these billboards—I'm determined not to have this propaganda ruin my trip.

Workers on the way home hope that some one with a car will offer them a ride. Most cars are jammed-pack with people, as are the backs of trucks. Horses are regularly used for transportation; it's not odd to see someone gallantly riding a pony, at a full gallop—while other horses trod along with two or three people on their tired, old backs. Burros are very common in the countryside—looking rather comical as riders bobble on their backs. Often, you'll see a mother or father pulling a donkey that's carrying a couple of children bareback on its hairy hide. Saddles are not easy to come by and, if you find one, it's going to be unaffordable. Some travelers make due with just a blanket on their animal's backs. Bicycles are everywhere; they're reliable to get you where you want to go, but if you get a flat you're in trouble.

It's five o'clock in the afternoon and the farmers are still working the fields. Plantain trees grow everywhere—as well as yucca, cassava, bananas, tomatoes, corn, avocado, guava. Mango trees abound with fruit. The earth is so rich, it's red in color—yet, people are hungry. Where does the harvest go? Who sells it and who buys it; most importantly, who eats it? Of course, the tourists have access to everything: you name it and they have it; the native Cubans don't see any of this. The buffets at the hotels are as grand as the ones offered in Las

Vegas hotels; but, sad to say, their workers are not allowed to eat the food they serve. The biggest crime of all occurs when these servants witness leftovers disposed of as garbage, while they are not given the opportunity to take food home to their families.

Varadero is an easy two and a half hour drive from Havana; we've been on the road for one and a half hours now—passing some of the most beautiful tropical scenery that I've ever seen: lush green valleys and rolling hills, with an abundance of palm tree groves, packed with coconuts. In the mist of this beauty, shanty houses dot the landscape—with goats, cows, and chickens of multicolor hues; including, arrogant roosters perched on fence posts, cock-a-doodle-doing to their hearts' content. Naked children ran around—playing and upsetting the community of the henhouse. (This brings back fond memories of my own childhood, when I would terrorize the chickens.) Mamá would get ballistic, because I would make the hens so nervous they wouldn't lay eggs. I was so bad then; eventually, my mother tired to the point of giving up the pursuit of controlling me. Since I couldn't get Mamá angry enough, I gave my mischief up and settled down. Then, I didn't drive the chickens mad anymore…I just ate them.

At the halfway point of our trip, we stopped at a roadside refreshment stand for a quick snack and a chance to de-fuel (i.e., attending to the rest room). The large wall-less hut consisted of a cement floor with an oval bar in the center and black tape-mended vinyl stools that had seen better days. Two bartenders graciously attended both busload of tourists, who were drinking beer and eating pork sandwiches. This was an international party, with everyone speaking in their native language—striving to be heard over the loud Cuban music in the background. Wild birds and parrots flew inside the hut—waiting for a morsel of food to fall on the floor. There were also plenty of dogs, chickens, and ducks around; and, they were all well-behaved.

I drank a refreshing Corona beer and took to exploring the area. In the back of this bar hut there was an old house tilting to one side; an aging, old woman sat on its uneven porch—smoking a cigar and rocking on an old wicker chair. The old woman yelled out, "Amigo, do you want your fortune told?" I chuckled to myself at the whole scene and yelled back, "No way, lady! I'm a stranger in these parts and I don't want to know if something bad is going to happen!" "You are a wise man," came from a strong voice on the other side of the house—a young woman hanging wash on the clothesline overheard our conversation and decided to put her two cents in. "Hey, stupid," screamed the old lady. "Why are you hanging clothes? It's going to rain later." "So what? So...the clothes will be washed twice; why do you care? I'm the one doing the washing." These two women were so engaged in their yelling match that they didn't see me make a timely departure.

Across the street was a view that any artist would kill for—that is, to put on canvas. All of a sudden, the enchanting music from "South Pacific" filled my ears. The scene was the instance of the discovery of the island of Bali Hi. I was engulfed in a mist—unable to look away. Nothing else mattered, except the enjoyment of this moment. Nature beckoned and I sleepwalked across the street.

I stood at the edge of the road. I was spellbound at the sight of green mountains and deep valleys; I never knew that so many shades of green ever existed. Before me was a rain forest teeming with all imaginable tropical foliage—replete with thousands of native Cuban royal palms, positioned like soldiers. A renaissance tapestry sky was backdrop to a beautiful lagoon—nestled in the valley below and reflecting like a green mansion. Tropical birds were flying high in the sky, while white cranes—with long, elegant necks and knobby legs—were wading in the water—searching for their fish dinner; all this gave life and movement to a postcard setting, as a gentle breeze lazily swayed the palm trees. I sat and meditated for a long while; I even said a few prayers, as rays of sunlight appeared through a cloud floating past the sun. It was the perfect moment to be one with nature; and, I was.....in the moment.

The spell was broken by the bus driver's third call for "all aboard." While in a trance, I had totally missed the first two calls. I hastily gathered my belongings and ran to the bus—which almost left me behind. I entered to a round of applause and, after taking a bow, took my seat. "Onward to paradise" I shouted. "Onward," everyone replied. If a couple of beers is what it takes to loosen people up and make them friendlier, I'm carrying a 6-pack with me—just like the St. Bernard tugs a whisky barrel around its neck.

Speaking of the old St. Bernard, I haven't seen it in decades. I imagine law enforcement has halted its rescue efforts, because they perceive a canine pushing alcohol as not a good role model for young children—and corrupting teens. I recall that this giant dog only rescues adults—caught in blizzards or freezing to death on top of Colorado's ski mountains. There were times when I was on one of those Mountains—wishing for Schnapps to warm me up. Where is that dog when you need him...doggy prison?

Upon entering the *Yumuri* Valley, the vegetation thickened. The bus driver drove slowly, so that we could enjoy the wonderful view when crossing the *Bacunayagua* Bridge: the highest structure built in Cuba, which connects two mountains. I wanted to stop and meditate again; but, this time, the driver didn't stop. To describe the view is to repeat experience; and, one should only meditate once a day—for relaxation, that is. If I do this one more time, I will meditate myself off the Island; and I don't want to leave—just yet.

The town of *Matanzas* was just up ahead—lined with beautiful buildings, by the side of the waterfront. *Matanzas's* wealth comes from its status as a deep-water port, where large vessels and larger ships are able to anchor; which makes *Matanzas* one of the most important and busiest ports in all of Cuba. The impressive "Caves of *Bellamar*" are a short distance—outside of town. It's a pity that I wasn't aware of this location, because I would have planned to explore. I'm a cave freak; I see a hole in the ground and I want to enter. The "Pharmaceutical Museum," as well as the "Palace of *Junco*," is also located in *Matanzas.* I can't see everything on this trip; but, it will be a worthwhile stop on my next visit.

Entering Paradise

"*Entering Varadero Beach*," exclaimed the bus driver—with enthusiasm. The hokey tourists all started to applaud. I was emotionally caught up and I accidentally joined in and also applauded. Now, I was feeling terribly foolish, so I decided to sit on my hands to avoid another uncontrollable outbreak; after all, I'm not a tourist—I'm home!

The bus driver navigated through the narrow streets of *Matanzas*, with surgeon-like accuracy—depositing travelers at their waiting hotels. Varadero Beach is definitely a bikini-cruising paradise! Uninhibited men and women— wearing the smallest of bathing suits—paraded up and down the strip with arrogant flair. These are Europe's beautiful people—with no hang-ups and feeling completely comfortable in their skin bags. The North American tourist—you can spot in a flash. The men are look-a-like cookie cutters—wearing baggy knee-length shorts and baseball caps. They have spent years in the gym, pumping up their upper bodies, while they hide underdeveloped legs under long shorts. The women dress in 1-piece bathing suits, full-face makeup, and put on tons of jewelry. Sometimes, a bikini will show its face. Cuba is the wrong place to exhibit your wealth. The natives are hungry here; and that kind of exhibition invites trouble. Men who wear tasteless, thick chains and bulky rings to the beach are just showing that's all they have; which, by the way, also attracts sharks. Jewelry shines underwater—so leave the diamonds in the safe depot box, where they belong. Then, you'll have them, when you get back home. There's no one here to impress—you even may help a desperate Cuban avoid a horrible jail sentence for attempted robbery.

The hotels are small, quaint, and they face the ocean; there are also plenty of restaurants and snack bars. Mopeds and bicycles are very popular here—they're a great way to get around and can be rented for very little money. This town was really jumping and I was eager to arrive at my destination—so that I could start my partying. The sun was setting and there was less than an hour of sunlight left, as I watched the town disappear behind me. There were ten people left on the bus to be dropped off and I kept wondering when it would be my turn. The large, pretentious hotels were next on the list and they were separated from the congested, happy town that I liked.

"*Sol Club Palmeras Hotel*" yelled the driver. "Last stop." The doors opened and I stepped out to retrieve my belongings and breathe fresh, unpolluted ocean air. Now, I can finally relax and unwind from the exciting time that I spent in Havana. The driver opened the baggage compartment and handed me the last and only bag left on the bus. I was the last one to be dropped off and it was starting to get dark— which meant that by the time that I checked in and freshened-up, I was already going to be stuck in my hotel room for the rest of the night.

I picked up my bag and it felt awkward; the handle was broken and it was not rolling right. I stopped to examine it and suddenly the number one thing that scares me the most when I travel just happened. My bag was lost! This isn't my bag! It's the same green color and the same type of bag, but it's not my bag! I started to panic and hurried back to the bus—terrified that I was never going see my things again.

"*Por favor, por favor, ayúdenme,* please help me," I pleaded with the bus driver and the hostess. "My bag, this is not my bag. Please help me. Everything I have is in that bag. Please, someone took my bag by mistake or it's been stolen. Please, please help me, I beg you." The bus driver tried to calm me down, but I was frantic. "My passport." I grabbed the driver by the arm. "My God, my passport, it's in the bag. My Cuban and American passports, with two thousand dollars, my hotel vouchers and my airline tickets, they're all in my lost bag. Oh God!"

The bus driver sat me down and assured me that he would do everything possible to return my bag. He called the dispatcher from his cell phone and asked if a bag had been reported missing. The dispatcher told him that none had been reported, but that he would call the hotels—in order of drop-off, in reverse sequence—to see if anyone had reported a missing green bag; he'll let the bus driver know as soon as something turns up. There was silence, as we waited for the response. The bus driver and the hostess tried to remember what bags were handed over and where. It was an impossible task, but the bus driver felt that my bag might be at one of the last two stops. I suggested that we take a ride to the last few hotels and investigate. He agreed and we were on our way to the farthest one first. We reached the first hotel and he got off to check—nothing reported. I was in a panic again. I could feel the blood rushing to my head. I was stranded in Cuba! A communist country! I'll rot in jail! America won't come to my rescue! My head was ready to explode. I have no credentials! They won't know who I am. I was a man with no name and no country. I should have listened to my friend, Michael, and stayed home. What am I going to do?

The bus driver answered his beeping cell phone and I was holding my breath in suspense—with fingers crossed. "Please God, let there be good news." The words kept repeating in my mind, "please God..." "We found it!" the driver yelled! "The bag has been found! We have your bag, Mr. Infante, you can relax now." I let out a sigh of relief and sank into my seat. "Want some water?" asked the hostess, as she patted my sweaty hand. They both knew that I had just been through the roughest time. The bag was at the hotel next to where I was staying; a German couple reported their green bag missing and called the dispatcher to report the mistake.

65

The German couple were asked to wait at the drop-off point for our bus—which was already en route to exchange bags. The frightened, young couple were as glad to see me, as I was to see them. We exchanged bags and I suggested that we open the bags in front of each other, so that there would be no misunderstandings later. Finding everything in order, we shook hands, wished each other well, and apologized for the inconvenience.

Hotel Sol Palmeras

I finally arrived at the *Hotel Sol Palmeras*—exhausted from this ordeal and ready for a martini. Check-in went quickly and smoothly; I sped off to my room. I tipped the bellboy generously and served myself a fifty-milligram blood pressure pill, two water extractors, and a baby aspirin; then, I collapsed on the bed—hoping that when I woke up, this nightmare had ended.

I fell into a coma-like sleep for a brief time, although it felt like I had slept for hours. The intense heat of the room awakened me—after only a half an hour of nodding out. I went to turn on the air condition-er and, upon closing the sliding doors—which were left open—discov-ered that it was broken. *"Oy Vey!"* I cried out—using a Jewish expres-sion that I learned from my friends back home. I immediately called housekeeping and they sent someone to start the air conditioner. Tall, dark and ultra thin, he was an exceptionally handsome man—about fifty years old and wearing a mustache that reached from ear to ear. He inserted the plastic card, which the front desk forgot to give to me upon registering, and, in seconds, the air conditioner hummed and started to blow air. While the room cooled down, I took a shower to wash away the dust and fatigue—as well as the suffering memory of the temporary loss of my bag.

I was forced to shower with tepid to cold water, because there was a lack of hot water in this five-star hotel. I also noticed that the air con-ditioning wasn't cooling. Here we go again! I called the front desk and complained; they said that they'll send someone up in fifteen minutes. The fifteen minutes passed and I angrily called a second time to com-plain. Mr. Moustache was back again—after keeping me waiting for thirty minutes. I was wearing only a towel to remain cool, when he informed me that this was as cool as it was going to get. "If it's this hot inside, it's twice as hot outside," he said—with a grin on his face, under his balding head. "All the rooms have the same cooling system." At this point, Mr. Moustache no longer looked as handsome as before, but when I stepped out onto the balcony, I realized that he was right; it definitely was much hotter outside.

I was spending too much time dealing with things out of my control; so, I wore the lightest clothing that I had and headed for the buffet room. It was nine o'clock and I was starving. My stomach was speaking in a strange language—unknown to me or anyone else.

I walked around the spacious lobby—searching for the buffet room. A multicolor water fountain, dancing to the "Tales of the Vienna Woods" waltz, distracted my attention—momentarily. I was drawn to a stool at the lobby bar, which was just a few steps away; there, I treated myself to a martini, before dinner. What a mistake! With this heat and an empty stomach, I was in for a quick, cheap high. But now, my stomach was screaming, "Feed me! Feed me!"

I got off the bar stool and floated down a flight of stairs—and entered the dining room. The host escorted me to a table, which was next to a cage harboring a large, green parrot; he offered me a welcome drink, which I refused. The host instructed me on the serving procedure and handed me a tray. The martini was now taking effect on my nimble brain, as I waltzed across the room towards the buffet table. Every one must have noticed how dizzy I was—at least, I thought they did. Roast pork, rice 'n' beans and yucca, smothered in garlic 'n' oil—they rule here. I took this feast to my table and commenced feeding my inseparable buddy.

My Feathered Friend

Squawk! Squawk! The caged green parrot was going nuts. The poor thing was just as hungry as I was; but I didn't know if pork was on his diet. I gave him a piece of meat and he ate it in a flash. He kept coming to my side, squawking loudly for more food. The parrot was attracting so much attention that a waiter came over and asked me not to feed the bird. So, I stopped with the morsels—much to the parrot's disapproval. It flew down to the bottom of the cage and fluttered about in a frenzy—splattering seeds all over my food. I ran my fork across the bars of the cage to quiet the bird down; then, the host approached me and asked if I'd like to sit at another table. (Here I sit—high as a kite, hot, hungry—and at war with a bird that wants my food.)

"Yes, I want to move to another table...if it's not too much trouble. That bird is giving me a headache...with its loud squawking." So, I sat there—drinking a quart of milk to help me sober up; I was in total disbelief of what has happened to me, since I've arrived in Varadero. I was in search of paradise and found hell. What else is in store? Is Cuba punishing me for taking so long to rediscover her? I now believe in Dorothy, when she said, "There's no place like home."

Feeling better—after downing a quart of fresh milk that tasted as if my mouth was attached directly to the cow's udder—I picked myself up, brushed myself off, and continued my vacation—with no regrets.

It was time to walk around and become acquainted with the hotel. Large and cavernous as it is, it did have a comfortable and homespun atmosphere. The cabaret was closed for the evening; but if I wanted to see a show, I could take a shuttle bus to the sister hotel (next door) and see the tropical review. Right now, shows were not on my mind; stepping onto the white, powdery sands of Varadero Beach was more show than I could handle at the moment.

On the way to the beach, there was a recreation area, with a huge free-form pool and a swim-up bar, nestled in the middle of a grotto. A Japanese bridge connected the two sides. Color lights illuminated the palm trees by the pool, where guests lounged and sipped those tropical drinks with little umbrellas stuck in a cherry, that's stuck in a slice of pineapple, that's wedged on the rim of a glass. The underwater lights of the pool transformed a late-night swimmer into a black silhouette, floating freely in the blue water—it reminded me of Esther Williams, the American bathing beauty of the silver screen.

The trail to the beach led me through a garden filled with flowers and seaside foliage. Along the path, dim footlights paved the way to the ocean. I removed my sandals and dug my toes deep into the powder sand. Although it was pitch black on the beach, I could see the waves breaking in the moonlight. White puffs of iridescent foam gently kissed the shore—beckoning me to enjoy the coolness of its waters. I rolled my pant cuffs up and waded in the white lace-like water—gazing into the blackness of the horizon. I was absorbed in my own nothingness and I lost track of time—as I walked the shoreline. There were no distractions, except the sound of the waves and the splashing of my feet treading water. I looked up to the sky and there was a beautiful sight— the best show on the island: millions of stars in the heavens, shining brightly, twinkling uncontrollably, like Christmas lights on a pine tree. They appeared so close that I foolishly reached up to touch one. The only thing missing in this picture was someone to share it with.

In the garden, I was surrounded by hundreds of fireflies. Some landed on me; they were attracted to my moisturizer. I didn't want to swat them, for fear of hurting one of nature's most magical insects. Many landed on my arm—illuminating my body; I stood and was mesmerized. A deep, raspy voice came from within the darkness, "You must have sweet blood running through your veins, Mister." I looked around, but I didn't see anyone. "You must have the odor of freedom, for the fireflies to befriend you like that." A match was struck and a hurricane lamp was lit. Two black Cuban natives were sitting in the dark, sharing a cigar. From the glow of the lamp, I could now clearly see the men. I assured the men: "If I had sugar in my blood, I'd be dead by now." They laughed. "And yes, I do represent freedom," "In that case, sit with us, and enjoy a beer." One of the men made a gesture to a chair. "Well, it's rather late and I'm tired. I want to get an early start in the morning. Thank you, another time perhaps." "Ah, come on, sit and tell us where you're from, it's still early." I pondered this for a moment: (Yes, it is early and they seem friendly enough?) "OK, hand over the beer, I'll sit with you for a while." "You guys work for the hotel?" I asked—simultaneously opening the can of beer. "Yeah, we work for the hotel as daytime security police; as you can see, we like to have a few beers on our time off, then go bathing nude at night." "Yes, I can see that you're both naked. I too, enjoy swimming in the nude, but I'm always afraid that a fish might swim by and take a bite out of me."

I sat with them for a long time—answering their questions the best that I knew how. They wanted to know about freedom, America, food, money, schools, government, cars, fashions, and how others in the world were doing. They didn't seem to get much information from the radio or television; they only saw and heard what the government wanted them to know. These guys got their news from the outside by speaking to tourists—and, they were ready to drop everything and leave at a moment's notice. Even though as police they get paid a decent salary, they will take freedom over paradise.

I tried to stay awake to soak up everything that the hotel had to offer; but I couldn't force myself to stay awake any longer. I had reached the saturation point. I opened the sliding doors to my room and let the breeze mix with the air conditioning. The August air that blew through the open terrace doors was cooler than the air conditioning; so, I stripped naked, jumped into bed, and passed out.

At The Beach

After a dreamless night, my faithful rooster alarm watch woke me up. It was 7:00am and I was feeling totally refreshed. I can't remember the last time that I had such deep sleep—where there was no dreaming or getting up in the middle of the night to pee. I felt great!

Breakfast? Yes, Breakfast! I'm feeling my oats this morning and I'm terribly hungry. Shower? I refuse to take a shower this morning. Call me, Mr. Piggy, if you like; today, I'm letting the ocean bathe me. Ha! I'm a real perky fellow this morning! Today, I am having breakfast with a crazy green parrot that I won't allow to terrorize me. Today, the aggressive bird is friendly, shy, and cooing softly. I guess he doesn't like eggs or he must have been severely scolded for the upset he caused last night. I think we finally became friends.

It's 9:00am and I'm already sensing as if I've lost a whole day. Wanting to be the first one on the beach, I took a towel from the room and headed for the sand. To my surprise, serious sun worshippers had already staked out their slice of the beach. The sun rises early in August and daylight stays around longer—making the days seem end- less. I know if I don't seize the moment, the moments will pass me by.

Unfurling my blanket—on the spot that I've chosen—near the shore—close enough to the water—yet far enough so waves won't reach me—I stood mighty in my bikini—scouting the European sun- bathers, wearing the smallest of thongs.

After ten minutes, I got accustomed to seeing sunbathing topless women and a few nude men tanning their buns. I dove into the water, without testing it, and it was wonderfully cool and crystal clear. No matter how deep I went, I could clearly see my feet at the bottom. I floated carefree on my back for a long time—riding the gentle waves, bobbing up and down, catching the early sun on my face. I was always good at floating. Sharks? Not that I saw a shark, but the horrid thought took shape in my mind and it was beginning to disturb me. I started to look around for sharks—realizing that by the time I spotted one, it would be too late, and I'd be dead.

With that thought in mind, I got out of the water and approached the lifeguard for some insight on the subject of sharks. "Are there sharks in the waters of Varadero Beach?" The lifeguard reacted like I had just told him a joke. "My friend, the only sharks in Varadero Beach are on land." (I guess, he meant it's us humans that you have to watch out for.) "The water is safe, go and enjoy it. There hasn't been a shark attack in years,"—he said, still laughing over my concern.

I didn't take his advice; so, like a coward, I stayed on shore. (It would be my luck today and a hungry shark would be waiting somewhere in the deep for me.) I went back to my blanket and greased myself up. I wanted to get the morning rays and not expose myself to the noontime sun. I closed my eyes and started the cooking process—when I sensed someone standing in front of me, blocking the sunlight. I opened my eyes and there was a topless girl bending over me, asking for a match. I didn't know where to look. Her breasts were obviously the main attraction, but I wanted to be cool and tried not to look at them. I tried very hard to maintain eye contact at all times. She knew I was having a difficult time pretending she had no breasts, so she broke the ice by saying "Nice pair, hum? Do you agree? I'm kind of proud of them myself." "Yeah! Great pair." I said. "They even have a little hair on them.' (I tried to make light of the moment.) She laughed, introduced herself, and sat on the blanket. "You're funny. You should have seen the look on your face. My girlfriend and I are from Germany and we're here on our honeymoon. We've been together for nineteen years and we decided to make it legal. You know, domestic partners, that sort of thing." "That's cool, congratulations," I said. "We wanted to smoke a joint, but we're out of matches. We'll have it some other time, I guess." With those last words, she bounced to her feet and wished me a nice day. I watched her walk away. Her girlfriend waved and I waved back. "Beautiful girls," I said to myself. "With long blonde hair, blue eyes, and bodies to die for, no one's going to suspect that these girls are gay!"—especially not the group of guys on their stomachs or the ones under the trees—with their binoculars discretely glued to their faces.

71

From noon to 3:00pm, the daytime star is in killer mode. Wise sun-bathers leave the sand and plunge into the pool; others get under the shade of a palm tree; most will sit at the bar, refreshing themselves with a cool drink, during the mid-day cocktail hour. After a few 'sex on the beach' cocktails, they pass out under a tree. I decided to do nei-ther. Drinking during the day is not my thing; I'd rather walk by the beach and do a little exercise.

David

While on a quest to find the ultimate seashell, I stumbled upon the *Melia Varadero Hotel's* swimming pool. I carelessly left my towel and tee-shirt on the blanket at the beach and my shoulders were burning from overexposure to the sun's rays. There's wasn't a soul in the pool—not even a guard. Today's my lucky day. This is my opportunity to sneak in and swim in my own private pool. I visualized myself swim-ming alongside Esther Williams—performing a Busby Berkley water ballet. We swam in and out of a rock waterfall, which was adorn with flowers and green plants—we were treading water like dolphins. I thought I died and went to heaven. A family with a couple of scream-ing kids entered the pool—shattering my dream.

I took refuge inside the built-in pool Jacuzzi. I sat quietly in the bub-bling water, being careful not to draw attention. I was alone—but not for long. Soon, a highly energetic boy, who had been making awful noises, assaulted the Jacuzzi by splashing, diving, and spitting water into the air and into my eyes—making them burn from the chlorine. I was so mad that he invaded my peaceful environment—but I was not going to give up my spot. I had taken enough of this—I ordered the boy to immediately stop splashing water and making awful noises. He sat still for a while and he was a bit embarrassed by my reproach. Every so often, he would look coyly at the water and then at me. Not wanting to make eye contact, I kept a scornful look on my face—demanding respect. The boy stared at the sky and slowly started to move his legs—being careful not to splash. He knew that if his legs came out of the water, he was sure to splash—and I was going to scold.

We both sat in silence—until our eyes met and I said, with disinterest, "Hi, What's you name?" "David," he answered, shyly. "And where are you from David?" "I'm from Belgium." "You're very far away from home, David. Do you like it in Cuba?" "My parents like to vacation here, it's my third time in Cuba. I guess it's OK." By this time, we were becoming friends and started talking about art, history, and girls. He loved New York City and hoped to someday live there. For a seven-year old boy, he was extremely bright and captivating. He told me that he spoke four languages: French, Spanish, German, and English. The boy totally commanded my attention—with intelligent, adult-like, conversation; I truly enjoyed this youngster's company. I felt I was surely in the presence of a child genius. (Never underestimate the little people!)

Later, I met his father, who was in the diamond industry in Belgium. I offered to introduce him to friends of mine from NYC, who were also in the same industry. Maybe, I'll make a commission! Imagine—coming to Cuba to become a diamond dealer—ha!

I said goodbye to my little friend and his family, and left the pool. Before leaving, I looked back and there was little David—splashing and diving like a humpback whale, sprouting water from his mouth, bobbling alone in the Jacuzzi. Kids will be kids—no matter the IQ.

On the way out, I grabbed a towel from an unoccupied beach chair and draped it across my burning shoulders. I didn't consider the towel stolen, since both hotels were owned by the same country: Spain!

Shark Attack

Beached near my blanket were a sailboat and a few wave runners. I've rented wave runners in Miami, Puerto Rico, and Jamaica; and, I've enjoyed myself immensely. I looked the sailboat over and considered a ride—when a blonde, blue-eyed Cuban man, sporting a Coppertone tan, approached me: "Wanna go for a ride?" I replied with an apprehensive "No," which sounded more like "Maybe." " Would you teach me how to sail and what will it cost me?" I didn't want to swim in the water because I'm scared of sharks, so I thought I might as well play above the water. "Sure I can teach you, it's easy, and it'll only cost you $30.00 an hour." Boy! That's a real bargain. Back home, it would cost $200.00 an hour. "Let's go. Lead the way, my friend; you've got yourself a student!"

We went to his hut and filled out the required papers—which held him harmless, in case of an accident. We put on life jackets and headed for the boat. Pedro gave me some basic instructions and we were off to the open sea. "Remember, keep your back to the wind and change sides quickly." I watched every move he made, so that later I could duplicate them. I had a great sense of freedom—sailing in the open waters. The waves would crash gently against the boat and, depending on the direction that we were moving, the boat was sometimes airborne over the large waves. Once, I almost fell off the boat. I must admit that I was experiencing a bit of a rush. I was holding on for dear life—even though the waters of Varadero aren't deep. I have no fear of drowning; I happen to be an excellent swimmer, plus I was wearing that cumbersome life preserver.

It was my turn at the wheel (so-to-speak) and we awkwardly changed sides. Of course, I banged into him, but I had no idea which side he was coming from; so...we sorta went the same way—and—well—bang!

I was smoothly riding out to sea—until I had to turn the boat around and head towards shore. I forgot to duck under the mast, as it swung to the other side to catch the wind; it hit me across the chest, sat me down, and knocked the wind out of me. One problem now...we were both on the same side of the boat and it was beginning to tip to one side. This is a big sailing No-No. We had to act quickly. My teacher took over the controls and I moved fast to the other side; this time, I didn't forget to duck. If I hadn't acted fast enough, I would have capsized the boat and Pedro would have been very unhappy.

Waiting to calm down from the excitement, and for the pain in my chest to pass, I left the sailing to Pedro. Now, I was in it for the pure joy of the ride. Pedro shared with me that he has relatives in Florida, who want him and his family out of Cuba; but he's one of those lucky individuals—living happy and well under the Castro regime.

"I have the best of everything," he boasted. "I run a business at a resort hotel on the beach of Varadero, and I teach tourists the fine art of sailing. Castro takes 20% of my total income and I can buy anything I want with the American and foreign money that I make on the beach. Last year, the government gave me half an acre of land, on which I built a 2-bedroom house, complete with modern appliances—right here in Varadero. My wife and seven-year-old son deserve the best that I can give them. I assure you; I'm not a communist. I believe in God and in all the Saints: Catholic, and African. They'll always have a roof over their heads and plenty of food to eat. I love Cuba and my casual beach life. Every day, I get to meet interesting people from around the world. I'll probably die here. As you can see, I don't look like I'm starving to death, do I? Besides, I get to live in Paradise!"

The sailboat was in high speed—skimming, and bouncing over the waves. I wanted to take over the controls and continue sailing, but Pedro said the water was not safe and that we were too far from shore and in grave danger, if the boat capsized.

Pedro guided the boat through a long wide turn towards the shore, changing sides quickly—this time, without getting hit by the mast. I looked into the ocean and watched as rocks, seaweed, and a school of fish rushed past us.

"A dolphin! Pedro, I saw a dolphin! Over there! No, it's over here. Look Pedro, look! Quick, let's follow it." Pedro can't believe his eyes— a dolphin in Varadero; how exciting! We got closer to the huge fish; no, the fish is coming to us! It's circling the boat! "Pedro, Pedro," I'm yelling at the top of my lungs. "Look Pedro, look!" This time, Pedro got a good look at the fish; he couldn't believe his eyes. The fish must have been at least fifteen feet long. Fear came to his face and I became terribly nervous. "That, my friend, is no dolphin," he yelled. "It's a SHARK!" "A WHAT?" I screamed "It's A SHARK!" The sound of the wind hitting the mast and the waves crashing against the boat drowned out his voice. I enjoy television programs about sharks, but I haven't really considered how I'd react upon encountering a live one. My biggest fear just became reality. I was turning cold and sweaty— at the thought of being lunch to a shark.

"Hold on tight," Pedro shouted, as he hoisted a red flag that warned the lifeguards on shore of the danger. "I'm going to turn the boat around to catch more wind and race to shore." At seeing the red flag, the guards started to evacuate swimmers from the water. Everyone on shore was watching us rip through the water. I was scare that I might fall overboard, but I managed to change sides—in the process, cutting my arm on a metal strip that's on the mast. Blood!—the shark started to aggressively circle the boat—and with amazing speed. All it had to do was jump out of the water and pick off one of us. It was probably easy enough; the boat was only two feet above water. I held on for dear life—we were speeding towards the beach, where everyone was anxiously waiting. Due to an approaching rainstorm, there was a strong wind blowing from the east; this allowed our boat to travel at top speed. We were twenty feet from safety—when a large wave swooped up the boat and planted us on the shore. My heart was pounding inside my chest—I rolled out of the boat and sat, frozen, on the sand. I was surrounded by tourists, who were patting my back and wishing me well.

While Pedro and I talked on the boat, we had failed to realize how far we'd traveled—and, all the while, we were being pursued by the hungry, eating machine. Reaching the shore felt like an eternity; when, in reality, it only took a few very exciting minutes. This is one adventure I do not want to repeat. Only my dreams will keep it alive.

"I told you this was my lucky day!" I said to the lifeguard, who was bending over me. He was the one who previously had so arrogantly told me to enjoy the waters of Varadero because there weren't any sharks in it. According to him, the only sharks were on land.

"It's not your fault, but I'm glad I didn't listen to you. In strange waters, you swim at your own risk; above all, you respect the ocean. As beautiful and inviting as she is, it's also home to many dangerous, cold-blooded things."

A bit upset with the sermon, the guard stood up and mumbled: "I'll never tell anyone else to go in the water. All right! All right! So this WAS your lucky day. At least, you're still alive and you've had a hell of an adventure."

Pedro was anchoring the sailboat and putting away the wave runners. The clouds were threatening the land with a severe storm; a crack of lightning and a roll of thunder made the earth tremble and the rains were released from dark menacing clouds that hovered over us. Everyone ran for cover; most ran back to the hotel. It was not safe to be out in the open; water is a good electrical conductor—who knows what's next. As I ran across the beach—covering myself with a blanket—Pedro shouted: "My friend, thanks for a most exciting day. It's been the best ride in years. I'll see you tomorrow!" I shouted back, " No you won't, Pedro. I'm leaving early in the morning. Have a beautiful life, my friend."

I was saddened that I had to leave a new friend on such short notice.

I would have enjoyed sitting with Pedro for the next few days, bragging about our shark adventure over a few cans of beer. I saw Pedro watching me from his hut—until I disappeared into the bushes. I waved, without looking back. Farewell.

By the time I got back to the hotel, the rain had stopped, the clouds had moved on, and the sun was preparing another spectacular, Kodak-color day. I soothed my exhausted body swinging on an old rocker, refreshed my inners with an icy-cold *piña colada*, and transfixed my eyes on one of the most beautiful sunsets that pollution ever created. I looked up at the sky and I became terribly homesick. I suddenly wanted to blink my eyes and be home—in a flash. Yes, I had a wonderful adventure, met lots of interesting people, seen stupendous sights; but, I was alone and had no one to share this with. I felt sentimentally lonely—and it had been brought on by the beauty of a sunset.

Sure—the lifeguard must have meant that the sharks on land are Castro's vigilantes and the sharks in the water are the willing Cuban natives, who confront anything in desperate attempts at escape from the island. Some make it across, but most do not. I cried during that sunset—reminiscing about the entire week. How I did all this in such a short amount of time and live to tell, I'll never know. Maybe, it was just alot of good planning and plenty of good luck—or—maybe, somebody up there likes me!

The rest of the evening was about packing and getting my papers in order for my return trip. I squared away with the hotel early, so as not to waste any time in the morning.

A Clawless Lobster

Hunger pangs brought visions of dancing lobsters to my brain. I remembered that the seafood restaurant was located near the pool, at the sister hotel, where I encountered the boy genius. I took the courtesy shuttle from my hotel and it deposited me right in front of the eatery. The waiter escorted me to a very nice table, but I insisted on being seated under a ceiling fan—by the window facing the ocean— for cross ventilation. (I quickly learned how to stay cool on the tropical island in the middle cf August.) For starters, I ordered a corona beer with lemon; and for my 'Last Supper' on the Island, I ordered a three-pound lobster with all the trimmings. There were not many people dining at 9:00pm; they must have eaten earlier and gone to see the first show at the Cabaret. The few people that were here were also dining on lobsters, so this must be the way to go. For our dining pleasure, three guitarists played nostalgic songs from the past; they played a song that I knew and I decided to join them to entertain the guests—another one of my many talents. Unexpectedly—and totally improvised—I picked up the microphone and sang a slow, haunting rendition of *Bésame Mucho*—much to the approval of the guests, who asked for more! The management treated me to my evening's first *mojito*. I asked the manager if I kept on singing and entertaining the guests, would he keep feeding me drinks for free? "*No, No señor*, you have a wonderful voice and the people like you but, you will be here all night and I will run out of liquor." I began to tease him, "You want to keep your customers happy, don't you? *Sí, señor*, but I must also make money for my boss." "Look, my friend, these people, out there, heard me singing and are coming back to the restaurant. Now, you'll make even more money; you'll see. The more I sing, the more they'll drink; the more they drink, the better I sound. *Comprende*." I was rubbing it in and he was getting flustered. "OK, OK, mister." He bent over and whispered in my ear, "I'll give you another mojito on the house, but please do me a favor, don't sing again." "Alright, alright, I promise not to sing. So, where's my lobster?" This was the most fun I've had with a waiter—in years!

The stuff lobster flambé made an entrance—upstaging my previous performance—it was so stuffed, it was obscene. There she sat on the table—all alone—waiting—and steaming—looking all red and juicy. I edged slowly towards her—softly whispering.....*Bésame*.....*Bésame* baby.....*Bé...sa...me...* my lovely crustacean. We were both an instant hit; it was love at first sight. I treated her gently—caressing her perfect tail—as I slowly ate her—with a hungry passion. "Is the lobster to your satisfaction, sir, or should I bring you a mermaid," the friendly waiter asked and smiled. "More than you'll ever know, my friend, but I can't seem to find her claws?" "Cuban lobsters don't have claws, but they do display a hefty tail."

It took an hour to eat her. Left behind was a graveyard of shells and tentacles, which were instantly replaced by a coconut-almond flavored flan, laced with a rum caramel sauce, and topped with a mint leaf. The dessert was so good that I imagined I died and had gone to Heaven. I can't help it, but I know I'll never get this again. I'm not apologizing—I had seconds!

The second show was scheduled for 11:00pm; I had just enough time to get to my seat. On the way out, I stopped by the lobster-filled water tank and noticed that none of the lobsters sported claws. The poor things, how do they defend themselves in the wild? Now, I felt remorse; perhaps the cooks amputated the lobsters to make the salads. "Oh my God, I ate an amputee!" What a macabre thought.

Ladies and Gentlemen...It's show time...Curtain up...Light the lights and strike up the band...We proudly present...For your enjoyment ...El Ballet Tropical de Cuba...Here they are...before your very eyes...the dancing beauties of Varadero Beach!

What can I say that would be different? Just more feathers...more sequences...less costumes...more topless showgirls. The show was great for men, but not so great for the women. The costume designers always undress the girls and dress up the men. Next time, Mr. or Mrs. Designer, how about showing some male skin for the ladies—and for some guys—too.

My stay in Varadero Beach had come to an end, as I downed the last drops of the sixth *mojito* cocktail. The stage was now dark and the audience staggered out—at the stroke of midnight. I, of course, was intoxicated by the *mojitos*, and I was one among the staggering drunks. The open-air shuttle bused me back to the hotel in less than ten minutes. Along the way, the fresh air felt wonderful, but it also made the effects of the liquor more potent. There was a perfectly round moon bouncing in the sky; I could swear there were at least six moons—as my head nodded up and down. The driver was not kind to intoxicated riders and raced through the narrow path—blurring the palms and flowering foliage. Even the stars seemed to be skipping across the sky.

It was a struggle getting off the shuttle, but I reached the front door of the hotel safely. I couldn't take another step—the world was whirling round me. Holding my head in my hands and feeling sorry for myself, I sat on the steps for about ten minutes and dozed off.

I heard the porter's voice calling me, "Can I help you to your room, sir?" I was so embarrassed at the thought of having someone help me to my feet and take me to my room that I declined the invitation: "No thank you, I think I can manage by myself." It was a good thing that it was early morning and no one was around to witness my accidental drunkenness; otherwise, I would have crawled into a hole in the ground and kept the early worms company.

I made it to my room—holding on to the walls—as if walking through a narrow passageway on an ocean liner that's floating on an angry sea. I managed to swallow four aspirins and threw myself on the spinning bed—and hoped that I would not meet the morning with a enormous headache.

The next morning, I woke up refreshed and rested—and, surprisingly, without a headache. I packed my few possessions and made my way to the check-out desk to pay the bill. My departure time was previously arranged and I had enough time to have breakfast and say goodbye to my fine, loud-mouthed, feathered friend. For some reason, the bird was exceptionally friendly this morning—as if he knew I was leaving and I had come to say goodbye. The parrot even looked somewhat sad; his head hung low because he knew I was not able to take him along to escape from paradise. Before leaving, I took another look at the parrot—for the last time. New people occupied my table and the parrot was up to its old tricks again—squawking loudly, making a big fuss, fluttering its wings and spilling seeds all over the place. I was happy to see the bird making new friends. It was also foolish of me to think that the bird thought I was special.

Everything was back to normal again—except for me. Cuba had changed me. Its reality forced me to grow up—and I didn't want to grow up. Growing up is like—well—aging; and I don't want to grow old. I promised myself that I would always stay as young as Peter Pan.....forever.....in Never-Land.....FAT CHANCE!

The Lovers

Paging Mister Infante...Your van is waiting to take you to Havana...We wish you a safe trip...And hope your stay with us was a pleasant one. I entered the van and sat in the middle section. Snuggling in the back seat were a young, very attractive couple—obviously, on their honeymoon; in the front seats, sat the driver and a young boy; outside the van, the earth and everything on the ground was moist from the early morning dew. The sun was about a half-hour from entering the gray sky. A misty haze bathed the land with pastel shades of blue and purple. The door of the van was still open and I lost consciousness for a moment—I listened to the sounds of gentle waves caressing the seashore. I wondered how refreshing it would have been to take a dip—this early in the morning—while everyone was still asleep. I'd probably be the only one on the beach—gazing up at the dimming morning stars. Someday, in this lifetime, I'll find the time to experience this kind of uninterrupted peace.

OK, folks, we're on our way to Havana and the José Martí International Airport—buckle up. The first stop will be Matanzas. We're running behind schedule, so time is important; we're going to continue onto Havana and the airport—without making any unnecessary stops on the way. I hope everyone has "de-fueled" (Gone to the bathroom, that is) and is comfortable. I hope no one has left anything behind, except your footprints on the sand.

The sun is peeking through the palm trees and morning is in full regalia; the violet mist has disappeared and taking its place are the long shadows of the trees—spreading across the road; sleepy tourists are now making their way to breakfast, while the eager youngsters are running to the beach, with surf boards in hand, to ride the gentle waves.

I like this section of Varadero Beach. It's alive with young people in bikinis and narrow streets—lined with colorful shops. Vendors selling food and souvenirs, renting mopeds and bicycles—for that early morning ride. This is the real Varadero Beach! What fun! What energy! This is where I had hoped to stay, but my friends back home recommended a restful vacation—so much so that they nearly put me in a nursing home. Even though I've enjoyed my stay in Havana, next time I'm staying here.

I was so busy taking photographs and enjoying the ride that I was completely unaware of the drama that was unfolding in the back seat—and another drama at the front seat—of the van. I was sandwiched between two parting lovers on one end, and a father with a son that didn't want to go to school, on the other end. Arriving in *Matanzas*, the couple exited the van; hugs, kisses, and tears were exchanged, as they said farewell. The young man boarded the van and watched, as

81

his lovely girlfriend disappeared in the distance.

He sat in silence—brooding for a long time. I finally broke the silence and started a conversation with a quote from Shakespeare's *Romeo and Juliet: "Parting is such sweet sorrow."* He looked at me and smiled; then, sat beside me. He needed to talk to someone and I was available—willing to listen. Meanwhile, the other drama in the front seat was heating up. The driver and his son argued about going to school and becoming a doctor. The kid screamed to his father, "What good is a degree, when you can't get a job after you graduate. I still have to work the sugarcane field every day, so I might as well make it my career." Of course, I had to put my two cents in by advising the boy that he should finish high school first; then, later, decide what he wanted to do for the rest of his life. His father agreed and everything was quiet again. The boy sat in silence—contemplating my words. Depress and choking on his words, the young lover began to tell me the story of his three-year relationship with the girl. Three years ago, they met in Varadero Beach and fell in love instantly. He's a student of law in Argentina and his father, a prominent lawyer, forbids him to marry—until he is an established professional, or else his inheritance will be cut off. His girlfriend's father—on the other hand—wants a better life for his daughter and is pressuring the young man to marry—or never see her again. The young couple are willing to wait for the right time to marry—no matter how long it takes. A long courtship is not rare in Argentina or Cuba; couples can be engaged for two to three years before marrying, since it's believed that this extended courtship helps make a solid relationship. The girl's father is impatient and won't hear of this; he wants his daughter out of Cuba as soon as possible. The Argentine lover is caught between the dagger and the wall; he's left with no choice but to obey his father. Unbeknownst to the girl, this is going to be the last time that she will see her handsome lover. He will write her a letter, as soon as he's back home in Argentina—explaining, why the relationship had to end. Cuban fathers can be very stubborn, but the combination of Italian, German, and Spanish, make the Argentine fathers just as hard-headed.

Being pressed for time to make our destination on schedule, the unpredictable happened. Smoke was escaping from the hood of the van and we had to pull over to investigate the problem. The fan belt had broken and we aren't moving another inch. The driver doesn't have a spare belt and we're going to have to wait for emergency repairs to reach us. Stress was building up—at the thought of missing the flight and getting stranded in Cuba

Twenty minutes passed and no sight of the emergency truck. I was ready to hitchhike, when the emergency vehicle pulled up beside us. It took another ten minutes to get us going. Exceeding the speeding limit, the driver got us safely back to Havana—on schedule. David, the Argentine boy, gave me a strong hug, thanked me for listening, and wished me a good life. What will be.....Will be.

I checked into the *Habana Libre* Hotel, which was going to be my home for the next three days. My room was on the seventh floor, over-looking the ocean, *El Morro*, and the *Hotel Nacional*—where I had stayed previously. All of Havana and the Capitol building were spread out beneath my balcony. The hotel was very comfortable: the room was spacious, with wall-to-wall carpeting, panoramic windows dis-playing spectacular views (especially during sunrise and sunset), twin beds, a television, and a bidet. On the lobby floor were several restau-rants, an open bar, souvenir shops, and the hospitality desk—for booking tours. The delightful, tropical swimming pool was on the sec-ond floor, adjacent to the breakfast room—which served a buffet for the morning and evering meals. I hung up my extensive wardrobe, occupying all of four hangers, in the closet and made myself at home. Within an hour, I was ready to explore Havana—once again. Only this time, I knew where to go—and with less fear.

As soon as I stepped out of the hotel and onto the street, the hustlers began to pester me. "I can show you Havana like no one has seen it before," said a well-dressed young man. "Maybe later. Right now, I'm visiting my family." I must have repeated that sentence several times, before reaching *Coppelia's*—where I proceeded to stuff myself with a hefty serving of vanilla ice cream. Parked near *Coppelia's* were sev-eral bright-yellow-colored *Coco* taxis (as they're called)—waiting to take brave tourists cn an exciting ride through Havana's busiest streets. *Coco* cabs are tricycle-like motorcycles, with one wheel in the front and two in the back. These cabs weave in and out of traffic (depending on how crazy the driver is) at top speeds of thirty miles an hour. They're great for navigating Havana's narrow streets. "Please take me to the old city," I said to the driver. He removed his cap—exposing a mass of long, luxurious blond hair. *"Sí, señor,"* she sang

83

out—with a 'devil-may-care' attitude. "Hold on tight, we'll be there in no time." All the *Coco* drivers wear similar uniforms; so, for a moment, I couldn't tell the guys from the girls. The ice cream must have been spiked with Cuban rum!

She's a pretty little thing, who asked a lot of questions, as she weaved in, out, and around cars, trucks, and bicycles—almost hitting a pedestrian. I held on for dear life—as other drivers shook their fists at her and called her a crazy woman. It gets even better when two *Coco* cabs race next to one another. The drivers will yell at each other, as they make their way around potholes; if they happen to hit a pothole, you can be sure you're going to fly out of the *Coco*—and your body will look like an abstract painting splattered on the side of a building. There are no potholes like Cuban potholes—due to slow repairs. The *Cocos* are rather noisy, but they're fun to ride; besides, everyone looks at you and smiles—they know that you're a tourist and that's also fun.

I had a lovely day—patronizing the same venues that "Papa Hemingway" visited in his heyday. There were pictures of him everywhere: at every bar, club, and hotel lobbies; and, not to forget, the obscene phrases written on public toilet walls about "Papa Hemingway." But, as they say in Hollywood, *publicity of any kind is still publicity.....and it's free*.

I walked the streets of Havana—not knowing where I was or where I was going. I only knew that— when I hit water—I had gone too far. I was back in Chinatown, watching an old man take a bath from a leaking water tank truck in the middle of the street. No one was aware or didn't care that this man was taking this bath. The man was completely ignored by passersby—as if this was something that people regularly did. I hid in the lobby of a shabby hotel and, from a window, watched the man take his bath—feeling sorry for his homelessness. He was doing his own thing, oblivious to the people or traffic around him. He needed a bath and that's just what he was doing: taking a bath—with his clothes on. My heart went out to him. I couldn't watch him any longer, so I took the pictures and left.

I continued my walk through the narrow streets—dense with people busily going about their business. The stores had some items for sale, although not much merchandise was displayed. Since the streets are narrow, it's very common for people to converse from one balcony to another—playing loud music. Some streets are so narrow that you can, on a good day, jump from balcony to balcony. It's one way to escape a fire. Most streets lead either to the Capitol Building or to the *Malecón*. The sea is a good reference point—to guide you around Havana.

I walked great distances and never got lost. After all, I am here to walk, discover and get lost. Discover what? If you just "look" at the sites, you might as well be on any other Caribbean island; but, if you stop and take the time to "see," you will discover that the people are friendly and the children are beautiful, innocent, and proud—even after enduring years of punishment from Castro's government. The land is colorful and fertile—just like the Cuban people are brave and strong—they still maintain hope for a better future. History unfolds before your eyes—through the architecture of Cuba's Art-Deco buildings and the cobblestone streets of yesteryear. Kings, Queens and Noblemen—as well as African slaves—have walked—and have been tortured and sold—on these Cuban streets—which were once thought—made of gold. And, maybe it was so—because Cuba has been raped of its riches by numerous unscrupulous men, who were hungry for wealth and power. There was always enough wealth available for the next ruler to steal.

I'm saturated with Havana; now, it's time to head for *Santiago*. I gathered my gear and—early the next morning—I headed for the airport to board a small aircraft that only sat fifty passengers; the flight to *Santiago* was one and a half hour. On the aircraft, I sat next to a young officer of the Havana police, who was on his way to visit his ailing father. He is allowed one week, every two months, to help work the land that his family owns. The land has to produce a quota in produce or it will be taken away. His older brother, the wife, and his son also help in the harvest—constantly working—in order to keep their home and their substandard way of living.

We're flying low, heading south, on the Eastern side of the island—which made it possible for me to clearly see the geography of the land. Within a half-hour in the air, I got a bird's eye view of Varadero Beach. By following the road map, I knew exactly where I was. The red, fertile land below—where fields of corn, sugarcane, and tobacco grow as far as the eye can see was a sight to behold. A green carpet of rolling hills—replete with Royal Palm trees that stretched straight up towards the wings of the plane. It made me sad to think that such richness and beauty brought hunger and hard times to its people. The land that Christopher Columbus claimed to have been the most beautiful his eyes ever saw—today—is the paradise from which many would like to escape from—including the young police officer sitting next to me. I gave the officer six power bars for his sick father—hopefully, to help better his immune system. The officer was very appreciative of my gesture and wanted to do something for me in return; he reached into his pocket and handed me his card. "My friend," he said, "If you have any problems in Cuba, no matter how big or small, don't hesitate to call me for help." We shook hands and I saw his eyes water—as he turned away to look out the window. His father was dying.

The plane followed the main highway, flying over the city of *Camagüey*, which is situated three fourth of the way down the Island, towards the province of *Oriente*. Here, the captain changed course and headed southwest, towards the city of *Santiago*, we passed over the famed *Sierra Maestra* Mountains, where Castro claimed his successful take-over. It was minutes to touch down—and, the beginning of my adventures near my hometown of *Banes*. I said goodbye to my police friend—who had made me feel a bit more secure, by offering to help if I had any problems while traveling through Cuba.

Santiago

Touchdown! Santiago! I've been traveling from city to city and visiting small villages on the way to my final destination: my hometown— which is slowly, getting closer. I could have easily spent the entire two weeks exploring *Banes*, but I dreaded what I might find there. That's why I approached this trip in reverse—by getting accustomed to the Cuban environment via taking the long route. *What is there in Banes that my family doesn't want me to know or see?*

Check-in at the *Santiago De Cuba* Hotel was a nightmare. The host at the front desk couldn't find my room reservation or my legal documents in the computer. At the moment, my stay in *Santiago* (and Cuba, for that matter) was totally illegal. María, the tour guide employed by the Cubanatour Company, made all the arrangements;

so—noticing that I was quite upset—she assured me that she would take care of everything—not to worry.

I stopped drinking diet soda and ordered a double martini on the rocks, to help settle my nerves. All my documents had been sent, via fax, back to Havana to be properly signed. This transaction would take two hours to complete; so.....I waited in the lobby—drinking martinis—on the house. María reassured me that all would be OK and that the hotel was upgrading my room for the inconvenience.

Everyone was very hospitable and eager to make my stay a pleasant one; but, I couldn't help thinking what a disaster it would be if I get stranded in Cuba with no American representation. Will they arrest me and throw me in jail? Or, will they think I'm a spy and hold me for ransom? I was getting melodramatic again; I must have watched too many movies in my day. María laughed heartedly when I told her what was going on in my mind—we became instant friends. "Castro needs the tourist's dollars," she joked. "He wants you to be happy and have a pleasant experience in Cuba. Besides, you still have your flight tickets and the rest of your itinerary in proper order. It's our error here in *Santiago* that we're rectifying. If this had been a serious problem, our government would have escorted you to the next flight out of Cuba and wished you well—and a speedy return." We both laughed and I lifted my glass to toast María.

The bellhop escorted me to a one-bedroom suite on the seventh floor of this fifteen floor "out-of-context-eyesore" of a modern steel skyscraper—it looked higher than it was, because the homes in the area were no more than two stories high. He gave me the usual room tour and wished me a pleasant stay. I was very impressed with the luxurious suite, with its giant-screen television and pink marble bathroom—a basket of assorted tropical fruits sat on the table near the wall-to-wall window, allowing me a picturesque view of *Santiago* and the imposing *Sierra Maestra* Mountains that surround the city. I contemplated the view—sipping on a beer from the mini bar.

It was 3:00pm, with scattered clouds and no rain predicted. It was a bit late to start my sightseeing tour of the city, but there was still plenty of daylight for a relaxing swim and a nap by the pool—under the shade of a palm tree. I deserve a little pampering after the stress of the day.

I hastily changed into my bathing suit and did exactly what I had planned to do: I slept by the pool for three uninterrupted hours. Brain surgery could have been performed on my head and I would not have known about it—that's how tired I was. I dragged myself back to the room and, although I had rested, I still felt as if a gang of gorillas had beaten every part of my body. I was hurting all over—hurting, but I was determined to get my act together and attend the "Grand Cuban Buffet" for dinner. I swallowed a painkiller, got dressed, and went for the food. Oh! That glorious food! I was starving; I had not eaten solid food since breakfast. Lunch had been a mere diet coke, three martinis, a beer—and a *piña colada* by the pool. Am I considered an alcoholic? No, I don't think so—maybe just stupid! Dinner was delightful. The food selection was what would be expected from a five-star hotel. I ate like the pig that I really am. The blood from my brain dropped to my stomach to aid the digestion process—which made me light-headed, tired, sleepy, and ready for bed.

I decided to forego the show at the cabaret located on the rooftop terrace. The room offered a spectacular view of the city—while listening to *Santiago's* best musicians. Instead, I preferred to say hello to my pillow and sleep for as long as it took for my body to recharge—tomorrow's another day—even if I sleep right through it—lights out!

I knocked over a glass of water I kept on the night stand, while trying to answer the telephone. "Rise and shine," María's voice boomed from the other end. "We're meeting in the lobby at 9:00am to begin the city tour. Wear comfortable shoes, we're doing a lot of walking today."

It's a good thing she called me; otherwise, I would still have been sleeping. I put myself together in no time and went straight to the breakfast room. I gulped down two cups of coffee, a butter roll, and a cheese and guava Danish—stashing a few extra Danishes in my backpack—for later—in case I got hungry. I was in the lobby in plenty of time. I introduced myself to a young couple from Spain—also taking the tour. We waited for María, who was on the phone speaking with another couple that had to cancel—due to a long night of too much boozing. "Well it's just the four of us, so let the fun begin!" We boarded a private van and drove towards the city. On the way, María pointed to places of interest, which we could explore later—on our own. María was very knowledgeable of the history of *Santiago* and had an answer to every question. Like Cary in Havana, she also knew her job well. We drove around town, stopping frequently to check out the views, while María enlightened us on the history of the area.

From the balcony of the *Casa Grande* Hotel, located in the center of town and where we stopped for a cup of Cuban coffee, I observed that life here was very normal: folks were quietly resting at *Cespedes* Park Square, under the shade of enormous trees—having lunch or an ice cream cone or just reading a book or talking with friends. Some were annoying tourists, asking for handouts. *Santiago* did not feel like a Communist city—there was no Berlin Wall separating anything. The residents seem happy—shopping, minding their business—as in a free country. The stores were stocked with merchandise for sale and the art galleries exhibited wonderful paintings of Cuban landscapes—painted in bright, bold colors—which would enhance anyone's home. Across the park stood the Cathedral—painted in yellow, with two bell towers and a larger-than-life statue of an angel that presided over the town. On the opposite side of the square was the government house; and, directly across from the *Casa Grande* Hotel, still existed—in all of its grandeur—the home of Diego Velasquez. Inside the mansion is an exhibit of original wood furnishings and floor tiles, which were owned by the Velasquez family. Many of the furnishings have been meticulously copied from the originals—by Cuban artisans—and placed throughout the house; thereby, occupying the same space that they adorned when they were new.

The ghosts of the past still inhabit the Velasquez house. If you stood very still and very quiet, you could sense them moving around—from room to room. These spirits don't know that they have died; they will serve the Velasquez house for eternity. Horses and carriages were driven inside a courtyard that stood at the center of the house. The private chambers were built around the courtyard—the fragrance, I'm sure, was not of roses. The first floor was Velasquez's office; the second floor, his living quarters. The house is a Pre-Baroque stone structure, with Moorish balconies with floor-to-ceiling shutters. It was built between 1516 and 1530, and it's rumored to be the oldest home in Cuba; there is also a house in *Banes* that claims to be the oldest. Velasquez founded the seven villas of Cuba in approximately 1511; among them were *Baracoa, Santiago, Bayamo, Trinidad, Camagüey, Santi Spíritus,* and *Habana.* Velasquez came to Cuba in hot pursuit of the great native Indian warrior, Hatuey—who was fleeing the Spaniards from Haiti. After his capture, Hatuey was put to death and the rest of the native population was condemned to forced labor or death; most died from disease brought by the Europeans. Gold was found in the mountains and the natives were put to work to dig it up. Many suffered extreme abuse and were known to commit suicide. In 1514, after the Taíno Indians died out, Velasquez and his men started importing slaves from Africa. This period is when the African culture was introduced to Cuba. *Trinidad* became the sugar capital of the world—enticing pirates to raid the area for its wealth. Cuba abolished slavery in 1880. But even after the War of Independence in 1895, slavery was still functioning in a quiet and subtle way.

In 1988, after placing a bronze plaque in the center of town, the United Nations declared *Trinidad*—a World Heritage site. The cobblestone roads of *Trinidad* are still the original—and a bit hazardous to walk on. You can sprain your ankle very easily, if you're not careful. I suggest a good pair of flat, walking shoes when you're in *Trinidad*— and that goes for the rest of the island, as well. *Trinidad* is surrounded by the beautiful and fertile *Escambrey* Mountains. Below *Trinidad*— in the valley—the vast sugarcane fields seem to go on forever—disappearing into the horizon. Throughout Cuba, 70% of the sugar refineries have shut down, because sugar production costs more than what it brings in through sales and imports. The sugar that is produced in Cuba stays in Cuba—for consumption. And, because of the rich soil, sugar in Cuba is much sweeter than anywhere else in the world.

Back in *Santiago*, we passed by many narrow streets dotted with shanty houses—the poor section. Unfortunately, every place around the world has its shantytowns. A tin roof is commonly used for these poor homes. I remember falling asleep, at the beach house under such a roof—listening to the raindrops fall noisily upon it. I wonder how we managed to sleep under all that noise; but we did—and it was wonderful. The *Santiago* natives—that is, those who have nothing to do— spend the day outdoors under the shade of a tree, rocking away on rocking chairs or lazily walking—carrying colorful umbrellas to protect themselves from the sun—and visiting with friends; others take care of business by giving haircuts and shaves on the front porch of their homes—for pennies. The children happily play tag in the street in their underwear or naked as the day they were born. I watched a little boy play in the dirt with a broken down toy car—a little girl cradling a hairless rag-doll with missing eyes and limbs stole my heart. She was playing "Nurse" to the mutilated doll. The kids are all happy as a pig in the mud, but Santa Claus doesn't stop in this town—as he did in mine. I'm thankful that Santa stopped at my house. *I remember being fast asleep, as Santa ate the special cookies my father made for Christmas; and the reindeer ate the grass and drank the water that I'd put under my bed, to help them on their voyage through the neighborhood.* Watching these kids play in the water-soaked dirt—with their bodies covered in dry mud—just broke my heart.

Next stop on our tour was *Santiago's Morro* Castle, which was designed by the Italian engineer, Antonelli—who also created the design for the *Morro* in Havana. On this marvelous one-hour drive through the lush countryside, we passed by many modest homes that were kept in good condition—by some miracle. We also shared the road with horse driven carts, which delayed us, but were fun to watch and wave to the friendly people. We finally got to the edge of the sea, where high above the waves stood the magnificent fortress. Completed in 1710, the Castle houses mysterious passageways— and drawbridges, staircases, and dark barracks with jail cells, where African slaves were shackled to the walls. As I stared out to the open sea, with waves violently crashing on the rocky shore, I imagined pirate ships raiding the fortress. Iron balls flying through the air, bombarding the castle, and the Castle's massive cannons firing away in retaliation. Sails on fire, men thrown overboard and drowning in the fury of the sea, ships sinking into the depths of the unforgiving ocean—this was my fantasy. I'm brought back to reality by the laughter of happy children on a school excursion. María urged me to rejoin the group and we drank a glass of guava juice—before departing the mysterious castle of *Santiago*.

We were speeding to reach the Grand Rock, before the clouds rolled in and obstructed our view from the top. To access *La Gran Piedra*, we drove up a long, narrow, rocky road—some 4,000 feet above sea level. Along the way, we passed orchid gardens and small coffee plantations. The natives of The Rock (they live up there) had set up fruit stands by the roadside and I made a point to stop (on the way down) and buy the tropical fruits that I hadn't eaten for many years. But— first—the Rock.

The driver delivered us to a mountain café, where we relaxed over a cup of coffee, prior to the anticipated twenty minute hike up The Rock.

No one wanted to admit that he or she was out of shape—as we started climbing the hundreds of steps leading to the top. I was one of those not in great shape, so I stayed behind with María, who was feeling a little fatigued—even though she climbs this Rock every time she has a tour. I was not about to get a heart attack in Cuba—especially at 4,000 feet above sea level—so, I took my time. I'm sure the ambulance would not have rescued me in time, to keep me alive. I climbed at my own pace and rested often to catch my breath—that's how I avoided getting dizzy and lightheaded. The last few steps to the top were up a vertical iron ladder that on humid days can be very slippery and dangerous. Finally, we reached the top and the view was truly spectacular—well worth the hike. We were actually standing on a monster rock that offered us a 360% view of the *Sierra Maestra* Mountains to one side and the deep blue sea on the other. The timing of our ascent to beat the clouds—which María had suggested—was perfect.

Gray clouds were closing in to the right of us—as the sun shone to the left. This contrast of lights and shadows is an artist's dream. Two young women were selling beaded bracelets—made from an assortment of dry beans—for a scant one dollar each. How could I refuse? I bought a selection of bracelets to bring back as presents—and add to their humble income. The fact that these women had to climb the Rock every day deserved a gratuity, as well.

Descending *La Gran Piedra* was easier and quicker; although, we did stop at several places to learn about nature's herbs—and to buy fruits, picked fresh from the trees, by the natives living there. I bought two mangos, six juicy baby bananas, a pineapple, and a *guanabana* (a white, wet, fleshy, incredibly sweet, heart-shaped fruit that's my favorite of all fruits). The only drawback are the shiny, black pits; but, if you love the fruit as much as I do, you'll tolerate them. *Look for guanabana, sometimes called Cherimoya, at gourmet markets and go for them; they're usually imported from the Dominican Republic.* I made up my mind that the fruits I had purchased on The Rock were going to be my dinner on this, my second night, in *Santiago.* I was tiring of Cuban fast food and I hungered for natural nourishment. We made a quick stop in town and I bought a pink cake decorated with blue flowers. Later that evening, in my hotel room, I placed all the food on a small round table sitting in front of the window that faced the mountains—and, with my bottle of *Legendario* rum, I gave myself a Birthday Party.

I have enjoyed—immensely—my excursion to this tiring location, which was once considered a meteor that landed hundreds of years ago; that is, until scientists discovered new technology to study rock formations and assured us—much to our disappointment—that *La Gran Piedra* is only a monster rock. *As a precaution, I don't advise anyone over sixty five years old to attempt climbing The Rock— unless, of course, you're super fit.* Now, it's Miller time; but in Cuba, it's Corona time—with a slice of lime. We made a brief stop to catch our breath—before continuing down the curving road. Our next stop was, and still is, the holiest place in all of Cuba: the Sanctuary of the Virgin of Charity (*EL COBRE*).

El Cobre

It didn't take long to reach *El Cobre*. But before climbing the hill, we stopped once again by yet another roadside stand and gave the locals a little business. I treated my new friends to a drink of fresh coconut water—straight from the coconut—and later, the merchant cut the coconut in half and scooped out the fresh coco meat—for our enjoyment. *It's so good, but so very high in calories.* With our bellies full of coconut water, we made our way to the sanctuary, by passing through the small town of *El Cobre*. The streets were filled with vendors—selling religious relics and hand-carved statues of the virgin. Some—I admit—were intricately carved, and I was tempted to buy a statue. But, due to their delicate nature, I was afraid it would not have arrived home in one piece.

At the top of the hill, we entered the basilica, through the rear entrance. The scent of incense and Florida Water (cologne) permeated the marbled interior of the Shrine of Miracles—where grateful believers donated hundreds of crutches, braces, coins, and medals made of silver, gold and other precious metals; even a piece of the Berlin wall was displayed in the glass case—to honor the healing of the sick, the protection of freedom, and the performance of miracles during great battles.

In 1916, the Pope declared the Virgin of Charity the "Patron Saint of Cuba." From the Shrine of Miracles, a white marble staircase led up to where the Virgin is displayed; this area is always bedecked with fresh flowers and continuous burning candles. In the center of the room stood a glass-enclosed, air-conditioned niche—enclosing the diminutive statue of the Virgin. She is dressed in a yellow, gold-encrusted satin gown and wears a golden crown with inlaid diamonds, rubies, emeralds, and other precious jewels. I gazed up at the Virgin and, in a low voice, declared: "Dear Virgin of Charity, I have finally made it to your doorsteps and the emotion of standing in your presence overwhelms me. I have unconditionally believed in you and your miracles. I have made this pilgrimage, not to ask for richness and greatness, but to ask you for health and well being for me, my family, my friends, and my loved one, and for peace and better understanding among the people of the world, during these turbulent times that have been cast upon us." I stood there motionless—contemplating the Virgin in total silence—not taking my eyes away from her—not even for a moment. I feared she might suddenly disappear and I would discover that I was not here at all—that this has been all just a dream.....a dream.....this feeling of intense calm.....face to face with the Virgin.....which I......for so many years.....living outside of Cuba.....held so dear.....to my heart. My promise to visit the Virgin, before I died, had come to pass; just like the Christians, who—rather than surrender their belief in Jesus—preferred to die in the arenas of Rome. No government, dictatorship, president, leader—or whoever reigns over Cuba—can ever erase the faith that the Cuban people have for the Virgin of Charity. Although many might disagree, she is a part of Christianity—representing the Mother of God. The Virgin of Charity will always represent Cuba.

"It's time to go children." *I heard the soft, golden voice of María above my silent prayers.* I took one last look—from the rear window of the car—at the cream-color, red-dome structure that majestically overpowers the hillside. Once out of sight, I settled back for the twelve-mile drive to *Santiago.* Once again, we didn't escape the peddlers—who were waiting for us at the bottom of the hill. I did purchase a few postcards, with the Virgin's picture on them, and a handsomely woodcarved miniature statue of the Virgin. I accidentally dropped the figurine inside the van and it broke in several pieces; so, I gave it to the driver, who promised to fix it and keep it safe. I guess it was not meant for the statue to leave Cuba—at least not on this trip. Perhaps the Virgin was protecting me from being discovered by the border patrol—back home. For now, I was satisfied with the postcards, as my souvenirs; besides, back home I have a 14" statue of the Virgin that was made in Spain—with glass eyes and real hair lashes.

My eyelids kept closing on the ride back to the hotel. I had seen and done so much in one day that I was totally exhausted. I planned on indulging in a long, luxurious shower and a three-hour nap—to gather strength to reach the buffet table and gorge on more Cuban food. Passing by a bakery I yelled, "STOP! STOP!" Suddenly, I was no longer sleepy. The astounded driver pulled up to the curve and asked what was wrong. "Nothing is wrong, I just want to buy a Cuban Birthday cake and give myself an UN-birthday party—here, in my homeland." The driver shook his head, as if I had something missing in mine, and opened the car door. The bakery had little selection, but it did have one pink birthday cake with blue sugar flowers on top—and I took it home. I was the last person off the van and everyone thought I was totally crazy. I will never see these people again.....so.....do I care?

That evening, I took my promised shower and my nap—but I didn't feel like going out. I prepared the table with all the tropical fruits I had bought from the roadside vendors, my fabulous bottle of rum (*Legendario, Elixir de Cuba*, seven-year brut), and my pink birthday cake. I artistically placed them on the table and photographed them—for a possible still life painting. I dimmed the lights, put on soft music, sang a very happy UN-birthday to ME, and went to town consuming all my delicacies from nature. After the fifth glass of rum, I passed out.

The Market

The next morning, I discovered an open-air market, not far from the hotel. By 8:00am, it was bustling with shoppers, who were buying fresh produce and meats—before the heat of the day spoiled the non-refrigerated foods. As a matter of fact, there was no refrigeration. The meats were placed on the countertops and flies swarmed all over them. A little barbaric and unsanitary; but again, this is Cuba—a poor country. Beef, chicken, fish, pork, goat meat—all were in the open air, covered with flies. Dogs fought over scraps that were thrown to them. How these poor people ate the food and lived until the next day was beyond my comprehension: the salad stuff probably had to be thoroughly washed; the vegetables peeled and cooked in boiling water. Fruits were probably OK, as long as your body was accustomed to digesting them—otherwise, they would cause stomach cramps and severe diarrhea.

A Case of Intestinal Flu

This very thing happened to me just before leaving Cuba and I had to be hospitalized in a clinic for twelve hours—with the most painful intestinal poisoning I had ever encounter, in all my living days—just from drinking a home made fruit-brew sold by a very nice woman from her window sill. I—wanting to share the wealth—bought the unforgettable juice. My stomach pains started shortly after and got continually worse by late evening, prompting me to call the hotel doctor in the middle of the night, who sent me to the clinic. At first, the doctors thought I had severe appendicitis and were afraid that it could burst while on the airplane—which would have meant the end of me. So, I was grounded in Havana, and was kept almost a prisoner at the clinic. I escaped early in the morning, without being officially discharged; no one knew I had left. The plane—and my only chance to get out of Cuba—was leaving late that afternoon. I knew the doctors had good intentions and wanted me hospitalized for observation, but that would have meant that I would have missed my flight to Cancún—and would have been stranded in Cuba—illegally—with no representation of any kind. There isn't an American Embassy in Cuba and no one except my friends knew that I was—indeed—in Cuba.

I spent three bed-ridden days in a five-star hotel room—in Cancún—admiring the ceiling—at a cost of two hundred and fifty dollars a night. I couldn't walk or turn on my sides—without experiencing major pain. Chicken soup and lots of liquids—not margaritas and tacos—were my gourmet meals—with an occasional toast with jelly, and a banana. The doctor in México was wonderful: he called on me at 5:00am, because I had complained of severe pain, and, by 7:00am, he was back to take me to the American Hospital in his private car. Ruling out appendicitis—after performing intensive tests—he injected me and started me on a regimen of antibiotics. Upon returning to New York City, my personal physician, Dr. David Baskin, continued the same treatment—for six more weeks. I wasn't happy, but I'm alive to tell the story.

Back to The Market

I left the dreadful market as fast as my feet would carry me; I hailed a cab and went to the city; I parked myself on the balcony café of the *Casa Grande* Hotel and sipped on a double espresso—checking out the activity in the square. I left my appetite back at the market, so food was far from my mind.

Restlessly, I strolled around the Hotel—searching for more centrally-located accommodations, for the next time I visit *Santiago*. I took the elevator to the roof terrace restaurant and made friends with two waiters and a bartender. They told me what to do, where to go, and what to see in the area—and to not miss the Cuban buffet dinner of roast pork, rice and black beans, yucca con mojo (a garlic sauce), salad (tomatoes, lettuce, and cucumbers), dessert, and coffee—for just $7, starting at 7:00pm in the garden. I made a reservation and went back to my hotel to change into something Latin-looking. That evening, at the roof garden restaurant, I looked very *Cubanisimo*. I was dressed all in white and sported a deep, dark, golden tan. I had an open shirt, a gold chain, and white shoes—with no socks. I soon realized—too late—that I was sending the wrong signals by dressing in this way; the wealthy dressed in this fashion during the old days and I was definitely out of place.

I ordered a double-strength *mojito* and swayed to the music of a live band, playing the old favorite tunes. This was my last night in *Santiago*, so I took extra time and thoroughly enjoyed every moment. I sat—replaying in my mind—all that I had done and seen in the last four days.

I guess the most important highlight of my stay in *Santiago* was visiting the memorial grave site of the founder of the Revolutionary Party: *José Martí*—Cuban patriot, poet, and scholar—and my mentor—who fought against Spanish colonialism—and whose birthday I proudly share on the 28th day of January—which made me a very celebrated baby. *José Martí* was born in 1853 and he died in 1895; he was 42 years young when he was killed—but not before establishing his name in Cuban History.

The driver was patiently waiting to whisk me closer to my hometown; but for some unknown reason, I kept putting my hometown off. The main reason for this trip to Cuba was to recapture my past and find my roots; yet, I found myself playing the cat and mouse game—taking the long way to get back home. I visited the tourist towns that didn't mean a thing to me—a lame excuse not to visit *Banes* once and for all—and get the whole emotional thing over and done with. Maybe, I was afraid of being disappointed. I might hate it; it might not look as beautiful as I remembered it to be—then, I'd be forced to bring home an ugly picture in my mind, which might change my life forever.

Santiago is a lovely city and I met many interesting people—but I was anxious to be on my way. A three-hour car trip from west to east, across the wide and hilly picturesque part of *Oriente* Province, was about to happen. *Oriente*, is completely different from any other part of Cuba. The landscape is open, with green rolling hills as far as the eye can see, teeming with Royal Palm Trees that group together in bunches—as if God planted them that way, all shooting straight up towards the sun. Very few palms trees grow by themselves; most of the time, they have a little friend growing next to them to keep each other company. Plant life of almost every species is found here, as well as the wild herbs used for brewing medicinal teas. Flowers grow wild everywhere. The thatched houses that dot the countryside surround themselves with an array of colorful flowers. *Bohío* homes abound in this part of Cuba; most are very beautiful. Cubans in this region engage in some sort of farming—growing tomatoes, cucumbers, casaba, corn, plantains, guava, oranges, figs, papaya, mangoes, avocados, and other tropical fruits. Many own their own pigs, chickens, goats, cows, and horses—which they use for transportation and field work. Most of the farmers are happy with this way of life and they make out somewhat better than those people who do not have a little farm to supplement their income—or food quotas. During the Christmas holidays, the neighbors get together and share their food in a great celebration. Traditionally, a pig will be roasted in an open pit. Fa-la-la-la-la---la-la---la-la!

We passed by the old city of *Holguín*, I have ties there, but it will have to wait for another time—another trip. The drive was going at a leisurely pace—to absorb the beauty of the countryside. Soon, we approached the gates of the *Rio De Mares* Hotel in *Playa Esmeralda, Guardalavaca*. This will be my home for the next four days. The hotel was spacious, with a walk-through lobby that led to a double-kidney sculpted swimming pool that overlooked the beach and cabanas. The open-air dining room faced the ocean, which helped to give this hotel its five-star rating. I wanted to have lunch under the thatched roof, where dozens of ceiling fans—revolving lazily—filled the room with the scent of sea breeze. No! I didn't have the pork this time; I had the chicken 'n' rice dish, cooked in beer.

My room had a balcony that faced the pool and the ocean, with a full view of the stage, where shows were performed nightly. I didn't have to leave the room to be entertained—I could sit on the balcony, in my underwear, with a bottle of my favorite rum, something to nibble on, watch the show, and shamelessly fall asleep. I must sound like a lush, but the truth is I don't usually drink. I don't do a cocktail hour at the end of the day or have martinis for lunch; I do have a drink or two at dinner parties, holidays, and on very special occasions. But when I came to Cuba, something snapped inside and I became the booze hulk. I'm not insinuating that I passed out every night from an overdose of alcohol—but a few more drinks than usual, I did consume. *Arrest me already! See if I care!*

A cool dip at the pool and a *mojito* cocktail at the swim-up bar was the thing to do. But, "What am I doing in the pool?" I asked myself. I had come all this way to splash in the blue waters of *Guardalavaca* beach and here I am in a pool, sucking on a drink, and speaking to a pimple-faced kid from Canada. I don't think so." I jumped out of the pool—slipping, sliding, hopping, skipping, and crazily beeping "a la Roadrunner "—onto the hot burning sand and dove into the blue, emerald-green waters that I had longed for. Although it wasn't the same beach that I visited in my youth—which is only two miles away—it is the same water. Luxury yachts anchor on the shores of this grand hotel—with its piped-in music blasting on the beach—and white untanned bodies sprawled under blue umbrellas—it's a sure sign that this is a tourist-only hotel. Although Cubans can work here, they aren't allowed to stay and play here. Nevertheless, it's a beautiful spot to chill out; and that's just what I did.

I fell asleep on the sand and I got quite a sunburn. Luckily, the waves splashing on my feet, when the high tide rolled in, woke me up. I showered, and dressed for the evening in white pants and a white *Guallavera* shirt—again, looking like Papa Hemingway—and enjoyed a wonderful dinner. I moseyed my way to the lobby bar for a drink, where musicians were tuning up for the evening show. I ordered a vodka martini and started a conversation with the bass player. The usual questions were asked—like, "Where are you from? How's life, in New York City?" They were a friendly bunch—especially after I told them that I was born in *Banes*. Most of the musicians were also from my hometown and they started mentioning names: "You know so and so?" I offered the musicians a drink—unaware that employees were not allowed to drink in the hotel. Booze is only for registered guests and so is food. The trumpet player put his arm on my shoulder and whispered in my ear, "We'd appreciate it if you'd get us a drink. Just go to the waitress and order a glass full of rum. She'll know it's for us and will serve it to you on the sly. Inconspicuously, you will knock on the stage door and we'll invite you in. I mean, if it's all right with you? You don't have to do this, unless you're comfortable with the idea. I assure you, you won't get into trouble. You're a guest here and they won't dare reprimand you. Hey, they need your business."

I enjoy a good intrigue and doing something sneaky and mischievous was in order for the evening. I thought of "Casablanca" and "Play it again, Sam;"—espionage—Cuban style!

The band retired to their dressing room and I did what was asked of me. The waitress and I became friendly—as she poured the drink. Here, I stood—holding a tall glass filled with rum—and I was beginning to consider the outcome, if I got caught feeding booze to the band. It's like the zoo: the sign reads, "Do Not Feed the Animals;" on the sly, I always fed the animals. Just thinking that the animals were hungry made me break the law. I was just trying to justify my actions, so I thought more about the consequences. *Musicians always need a perk-me-up, so they can play better—and if they're terrific, it makes the hotel look better—I guess I'm doing a good thing.....WHO AM I KIDDING?*

I knocked softly on the door and I was let in. Every one was happy to get their alcohol fix—making me their instant hero. They were tuning up their instruments and the pianist heard me sing a few bars of

Bésame Mucho. He rolled his eyes, with a big smile on his face, as though he had just discovered a big secret—"Just as I thought! You're a singer, an entertainer? I knew you were an artist, as soon as I saw you. I just knew it! Will you sing tonight with the orchestra?" I was obviously flattered, but I declined: "tomorrow night, maybe. I like to be in control of my senses when I perform; otherwise, I forget the lyrics. Tonight, I'm just having fun." A baritone voice, sounding much like that of a circus ringleader—is heard above the blaring trumpets—announcing—"*Ladies and Gentlemen, it's SHOWTIME!*" I scooted out of the dressing room and found my place in the audience. The piano player made an announcement, "*We want to dedicate this show to a friend and fellow showman from New York City, born in Banes, Cuba, JOEY INFANTE.*" And I wanted to add: *AND RUM RUNNER FOR THE BAND!* Not expecting this introduction, I was slightly embarrassed. *Between us, I must confess that I did enjoy the adulation.* The show lasted for two hours, with the usual singers and dancers, feathers and smoke; after the show was over, the guests were encouraged to stay and dance for an extra half hour to live music. The trip from *Santiago* "did me in" and I was falling asleep in my chair—so I retired to my chambers; forty-five minutes later, I was watching another extravaganza—the one going on under my eyelids.

Earlier that afternoon, I had made arrangements with a private driver to take me to *Banes*. We negotiated a flat fee and he was mine for the entire day—to do and go—wherever and whatever I wanted to do—and anything else that came to mind. I was anxious to get on this road to discovery. I kept reminiscing, as I gathered the list of family names and addresses, and the places I remembered from my childhood memories—and now wanted to re-visit. What if I find something I don't like? What if I'm disappointed with the place where I was born? What if my family was dirt poor and lived in a shabby house? Will the people be uneducated, poor, dirty, and unfriendly? All the "What ifs" swirled around in my head and that was probably the reason why I took the long way to get here. *I was in fear of finding out the truth.*

Before tackling my hometown, I wanted to get a feeling of how others lived throughout this region: their lifestyle. I figured that by acclimating my eyes to the environment of these other places I had visited, this would soften the blow of what I might encounter in *Banes*. I've witnessed the beautiful mansions, the simple homes, and the shabby housing; the people that I've met en route have been very instrumental in helping me appreciate the simple life.

Today is a hot and sunny day and—for the rest of the week—it's expected to be cloudy, with heavy periods of rain. I took advantage of this clear beautiful day, snatched my backpack—which contained my bathing gear—and dashed off to *Guardalavaca*: the beach from my childhood. Again, I was keeping *Banes* on hold—for another day.

Guardalavaca Beach in Banes

The first thing was to find the giant rock that sat at the edge of the beach. It was my favorite place to swim and play games. Gangs of fish would come to feed on the rock's algae; I would be surrounded by hundreds of playful, tiny fish—as they fed on pieces of bread that I held under the water. As a child, I would climb the rock and dive off into the water—of course, to the tune of mother screaming, "Get that kid off the rock!" The water was only three feet deep at high tide and, during the low tide, one could walk out about a quarter of a mile in waist-high water. I was always a good swimmer, but I would scare Mamá to death whenever I would play "drowned."

The beach was overcrowded with locals—on picnics. I hung my backpack on a tree limb—next to a thatched-roof, open-air restaurant; this will serve as my landmark, so I can find it again, unless it's stolen. I had nothing of value in the bag, so if I didn't find it on the way back, it was OK; I would only be missing an old bag and a hairbrush. Stealing is not a pastime here; this is a family beach—known only by the locals—the people who have moved on, but are now visiting, and a few beach explorers. *Cuello Pesquezo* (The neck, as the rock was known) resembles a long neck with a protruding chin, holding up half a head with grass growing at the top—giving it hair. I splashed south in search of the landmark rock and found nothing but more sand. I asked a few older men, who were playing checkers, if they knew of the rock. They pointed north, without disturbing their game. I was sure these aging men remembered the rock from their young days, so I went splashing north. All I found was a sunburn—which required an occasional dip in the water to cool off and stop the burning. I was disappointed at not finding the rock, but I didn't give up.

Perched on a coral cliff, facing the ocean on the north end, was a fancy restaurant called *El Ancla* (The Anchor)—*which I recommend highly*—that specializes in seafood. I saw no trails leading to the restaurant from the beach; but since mountain climbing is a hobby of mine, I managed to scale the coral rock, reaching the top—but not before staring at a pair of black construction boots standing in front of me. Precociously, I looked up at the somber, angry face—looking down on me with pressed lips. The giant guard pulled me up to solid ground—after I explained who I was and what I was doing there. "Well," he said, "The rock you're looking for is imbedded in the sand, near the scuba center. You can see it from here." What a disappointing piece of rock: eighteen feet wide by twenty-five feet long and about fifteen feet high, with grass and a small tree growing on the top. The guard told me, that by popular demand—for the nostalgia seekers, *like me*—the rock was going to be excavated and placed in the water—again. The caretaker, looking more menacing than his bite, showed me an easier way down the coral cliff; this took me back to the beach and to the rock.

I touched—rubbed—patted—even kissed and hugged—the rock. I had some reservations about *this* being the "Rock," but I have to believe the word cf the seniors, who have lived here their entire lives. OK.....OK.....nothing stays the same for very long. It's been more than half a century, since I've been back. How can I be so selfish as to expect life to remain the same? Although, this area has in many ways stayed the same: the water is still purple, green, blue, and turquoise; the sky is a soft tiffany blue, except when it's cloudy and angry, then it cries for a short time, and when the clouds empty out their tears, they move away—exposing a sun so bright that it blinds the eyes.

I snuggled under a tree—its branches cast a giant, embroidery-like purple shadow on the sand. I listened to the strumming of a guitar playing in the distance—in harmony with the sound of the waves kissing the shore. I rested.....

With the addition of several new restaurants and luxurious hotels, *Guardalavaca* appeared the same; a place that is enjoyed by locals—and less tourists. My driver was waiting, where he had left me earlier that day to drive me back to the hotel—where a late afternoon tour was waiting to escort me to another town. It didn't take long to reach the historical, picturesque, ocean-side town of *Boca de Sama*—where

I was shown—first-hand—how Cubans bought their rationed merchandise. A wild—'at your own risk' stroll—on a razor-sharp coral reef, once underwater—proved worthwhile—just to watch a fisherman harpoon his dinner with amazing accuracy: he speared his fish, walked barefooted on the reef, and was able to avoid getting his feet and body cut and mutilated by these very rocks—which had sunk many a ship and had now split the rubber soles of my sandals in two. Next, en route, was a working farmhouse—equipped with everything living and everything growing—including chickens, turkeys, pigs, goats, cows, and horses—all running loose with no fences or corrals to enclose them. Bananas, papaya, coconuts, guava, plantains, mangoes—if it grew on a tree, it was here. I sampled everything that was ripe and ready to eat. The lady of the farm served our group a demitasse of espresso coffee, which had been brewed from local beans. For me, she prepared a cup of coffee made with freshly-boiled goat's milk— that was taken directly from a goat tied up at the back of the house. I was raised on goat's milk—the gesture was very special. Before leaving, I kissed the goat for its participation on this occasion and gave the woman a few bucks for her trouble—which she gladly performed. It was the perfect ending to a perfect day.

It was nearly dark when I got back to the hotel—tired, sloppy, and grumpy. I sat at the bar and nursed a rum martini—to mellow out. This was the first hard liquor I've had throughout this whole trip. *OK.....I lie.....Shoot me!* I ordered dinner at the bar, knowing very well that if I went to my room to freshen up, I'd never leave it—and I was right! Before reaching the door to my room, my shirt was off, my belt unbuckled and I was holding one shoe. I took the quickest shower in history and—soon—I was swallowed in darkness.

The following morning, I sleepwalked through a breakfast of fried eggs and ham, bread and butter, a big dish of sliced tropical fruits— and two cups of espresso coffee—to wake me up. I wrapped up a few danishes and a couple of sesame rolls to share with my driver—during our excursion to *Banes*. This was going to make him happy—food of this sort is a delicacy for the people, who are not permitted to eat at the hotels.

My backpack was over my shoulder again and, with squinting eyes, I stepped into the bright sunlight to meet my driver. Sunglasses would have been appropriate, but I like to see the world in its natural colors.

The taxi attendant beeped my driver and, in two minutes, the car pulled up—freshly washed and vacuumed—with the air-conditioning on high. It was 9:00am and it was already extremely hot. *I can only imagine how hot it's going to be by noon.*

"My name is Pinto, at your service, *Señor Infante*. Are you ready for your tour?" "Yes," I replied—looking at him inquisitively. Pinto? What a crazy name. His face was discolored, with white and brown spots—as in—missing pigmentation. There was a similarity with Pinto's face and that of a Pinto Pony; that's probably why his friends lovingly called him Pinto. I pictured how strange he must look in the nude—all spotted. But, beauty is in the eye of the beholder. Yet, he was a very handsome man, soft spoken, medium built, and about forty-five years old. I handed him a list of addresses and places that I wanted to visit. "Yes, I'm ready for my tour. Do you know the areas that I want to visit?" Pinto nodded his head in affirmation, "Yes, and it's not difficult to find these homes; I'm also from *Banes*." What a blessing—not only do I have a pleasant driver, he also lives in my hometown. This makes everything so much easier. GOD must have sent this man to me; I'm sure of it— I'm sure that GOD has been guiding this whole trip, step by step. I don't really think I could have done it on my own. Everything is falling into place like clock work; I truly believe that a higher power has been protecting me from harm's way. This superior force has been my traveling companion—I somehow knew where to go, without knowing the way. This may sound like the *Twilight Zone*, but I do believe in the afterlife—and, the superior guidance of the spiritual world.

The two way, one lane road to *Banes*, was partly paved—and the part that wasn't had enough potholes to sink a battle ship. There were no sidewalks; people walked on the side of the road or followed a narrow dirt trail, usually one in back of the other—a la hillbilly style. The countryside is as beautiful, as described in the tour books. Emerald green-colored rolling hills stretch as far as the eye can see, with clusters of Royal Palms rising majestically towards the sky. Bohio-type homes, nestled under giant-leafed banana trees, were surrounded by tall cactus hedges—dense enough that one can actually stand on top of them without falling through. Poor is the name of the game in this part of Cuba; simple living is the way to go. The black market is not as prevalent here, as it is in Havana and *Santiago*. People here depend solely on the government rations that are given to them—and whatever extras they can harvest themselves. Yet, it's paradise to the eye—if you don't need to eat to survive.

Up ahead, I saw the sign written on an archway that read, "ENTERING BANES." My heart jumped a beat or two—palpitating with anticipation—all my senses were on high alert. My eyes were registering everything they saw—I didn't want to miss a thing. I put my head out the window to feel the temperature of the region and smell the air—like dogs do, when they sit in a car with their heads out the window. The air was fresh and unpolluted, with the fragrance of honeysuckle. I was beginning to relive the past. But still, I was holding back from reaching my final destination. I was apprehensive, so I suggested to Pinto to steer towards another beach that I had enjoyed as a child—and stop for lunch. As I recall, *Playa Puerto Rico* is a raw stretch of wild beach—kissed by turquoise waters—producing medium-size waves that rush the shore, leaving fan-shaped foam on the sand, which quickly disappears back into the sea; round, green-leafed trees line the beach and curve their branches down, resting them upon brightly-color shells; yellow-green seaweed adorns the coast. The giant blue crabs make their home here; they dominate the region; during the mating season, their sharp claws have been known to puncture car tires—leaving stranded those brave souls that dare to venture into blue crab territory.

Swerving side-to-side to avoid the massive potholes, we made our way to the beach; which—now—looks completely different. Run-down beach homes that once were elegant summer homes lined a large strip of the raw beach—the beautiful sea shrubs and palm trees, whose trunks bent towards the sea, no longer are there. Everything has been taken over by land developers, who—for profit—had increased the size of the beach—only to fall into disrepair after the downfall of the Soviet Union—and the tourists stopped coming. All its natural beauty had been taken away. I recognized NOTHING—and this dream has been rudely shattered. I had no desire to walk on the beach in search for the giant conch shells—or for the long-awaited dip in the ocean. It was a different place—another time

The restaurant (or *Paladar*) was located in one of the shanty homes, and was slightly leaning to one side; it has a family-style dining room and a large wooden table that sat eight people on two long benches. Conch shells and fishing nets decorated the driftwood fence placed around the shack. Outside, under a thatched roof was the beach bar—tree stumps served as tables and chairs. We sat with beer in hand, while our chicken and rice lunch was being prepared. Meanwhile we were entertaining ourselves by watching two kids poking a stick into a hole in the sand, trying to coax a tarantula spider out of its home. They would poke the hole and run, then poke again and run. I used to do the same 'stick thing' in my day—and ran like hell, when the first 3 hairy legs poked out of the hole. *At least, something is still the same.*

Lunch was served: tree-picked creamy avocado salad, with sliced onions, sprinkled with Spanish olive oil and lemon juice; followed by thin, crispy, fried plantains with a green garlic sauce for dipping—and the best chicken 'n' rice dish with *chorizos* and saffron I had ever tasted. Back home, I get rave reviews from my friends when I make my version of chicken 'n' rice. I follow Mamá's recipe; but through the years, it has become "Americanized," by using vegetable oil—instead of the artery clogging *manteca* (or lard) that makes Latino dishes so flavorful. The chicken 'n' rice portions were gigantic, but not a grain of rice was left on the plates. I was completely satisfied and fulfilled—like a pig in mud. The cost for all this food was a mere $7 for two people, including espresso coffee and a dish of rice pudding. It made me feel like I was taking candy from a baby—I felt so guilty that I left them a twenty.

It was now the long awaited time to face my town—the hours were ticking away and this was the only day I had to complete this trip. Entering the wide downtown strip, with rows of empty stores with broken windows, I couldn't recall a single landmark. I can still picture the streets—highly decorated for Christmas—with their colorful windows full of toys and wonderment—folks would be happy, laughing, joking, shopping, and gossiping. To this day, I can still feel Mamá holding my hand—and me trying to get loose. But her grip was always stronger than my pull. *Overprotected? Yeah, I probably was.*

Banes

Nowadays, the strip has a few government stores opened and a couple of individually-owned stores that pay high taxes—keeping the owners just as poor as they were before, when they didn't have to work so hard. The remaining population depends only on the rations that the State supplies and the help they receive from families living abroad, if they are lucky enough to have someone living on the outside.

A sudden wind blew dust up from the ground and covered us with dirt—reminiscent of a ghost town of Western America in the middle of a tumbleweed-filled prairie. As we continued along the road, we arrived at the towns square, *Parque Dominguez;* where, in the center, stands the band shell—which now sports a cracked cement floor and graffiti pillars. The four *flamboyán* trees—two on either end of the park—no longer bloom. I asked Pinto to park the car; I wanted to be by myself and cry.

I strolled around the park—in disbelief of what had become of this beautiful place. Trying to see *Banes* as it was, I squinted my eyes to filter reality—but the illusion did not work. The liveliness of this space, which once generated great energy, is now gone. I sat uncomfortably on a broken bench and daydreamed the park—as it once was. Slowly.....the ghosts of the past began to replay in my mind's eye.....the park was alive.....for me.....once again. I heard the band playing.....I saw couples dancing.....I heard the chatter of the townspeople.....the laughter of happy children.....I even saw myself—climbing trees. For an instant, I had escaped into a cellophane dimension that was slowly materializing—when I heard Pinto's voice—reminding me of the time—the spell was broken—the ghosts evaporated into the past and I was left—once again—with the ugly reality. The theater *Dominguez* is now a dishevel discothèque; the balcony where I went for ice cream and sodas is closed and considered dangerous. Also in ruins—from a lack of desperately needed tools and supplies—are the once-elegant estates that surrounded the park. At one time, the proud and pretentious middle-class homeowners would keep their centrally-located properties meticulously painted and professionally-manicured. Back then, the houses were scrutinized daily—by neighbors and tourists, who used the park for socializing or just to relax under the shade of a tree.

Stationed on the other end of the park was a truck playing loud music; the town's bum danced with his favorite partner—a popular, no-label bottle of rum. The town's bum was gone to the four winds; he was having the time of his life. I figured—that he figured—that life was too short and Castro would survive him anyway—sooooo, why not indulge. He drank in celebration of having nothing to do and nothing to look forward to; he was also a nuisance to a couple of men who were playing an intense game of Dominos—a favorite pastime for Cubans. One man kept pushing the bum gently away; but the bum kept coming back, slurring insults at the man—until—finally—the man had enough abuse. He stood up, tall and menacing, shaking his fist at the staggering man—who kept backing up and turning in circles. Seeing a fist go up, ready to strike, the babbling, homeless man— untouched—dropped to the ground in utter defeat. Everyone—including me—laughed at the intoxicated clown.

The park had been another disappointment. Directly across the street, and in shambles, was "The Cuban Club" or *Club De los Gallegos.* The building had been stripped of its marble facade and marble columns, which once decorated its entrance. The plaque had also been removed—leaving a stain on the wall from where it once hung. Only the name of the club—inscribed in mosaic on the entrance floor—had been left untouched. The antique, carved, wooden doors were decayed, and the front stain-glass windows were all cracked and boarded up. I found an opening and peeked inside—expecting the worse. I couldn't believe my eyes...Where were the marble walls and shiny floors?.....the pedestals—where huge flower arrangements sat?...the palm trees?.....the mirrors and the golden wall sconces?.....the crystal chandeliers?.....the lace tablecloths and silverware?.....the Luis XV brass-decorated furniture?.....the Spanish-carved high-back chairs—upholstered in red velvet with gold tassels?.....The paintings and French draped curtains? Barely visible was a small portion of the hand-painted ceiling; where was everything now? Obviously—not here! Inside was desolation, dust, decaying walls, wood planks on the floors, shattered multicolor glass from the stain-glass windows—police barricades occupied the room for storage and a basketball hoop replaced the giant mirror. "This is our gym," said a young boy. "Would you like to go inside?" For an instance, I was startled. I was faced by a pair of giant-size blue eyes—smiling up at me—with the blackest, furriest lashes that I had ever seen. The boy looked as if he was wearing eyeliner—due to the thickness of his lashes. "Sure! I'd like to go inside, you lead the way." He grabbed my arm and suggested we go in through the back, where there was a hole in the wall, which we could—maybe—squeeze through. His name was José (the same as mine), and he was eleven years old. In Castro's regime, a boy of this age would not be considered innocent. These children quickly grow up by learning the game of survival. The thought of possibly falling prey to a gang of street kids—waiting in the back—sat uneasy in the back of my mind. I must admit—I was hesitant—but I followed José anyway. We reached the backyard by way of an alley way; there, he was greeted by two younger boys, who were sitting on the steps sharing a cigarette. My first impression was "Yep, there's the gang!" But, the boys quickly disappeared. José found the opening in the wall; but, unfortunately, it was too small for my body to crawl through. I was flattered that José had not considered my bigness. "This patio was the garden section of the club," I explained to José—who had no idea what this place was—or stood for. "This building—I continued to explain—had white marble tiles, with large ceramic planters filled with palm leaves. Exotic flowers were everywhere you looked and, placed in the four corners of the garden, were ornately-carved, white-stained wooden benches and a row of white, wicker, peacock chairs—facing the babbling brook. Nothing from those days is here today. I wish you could have seen it then, little Joe." How was it possible for me to think that all my dreams would still be here waiting to be discovered—after all these years? José noticed that what he had shown me had saddened me, so I explained my odyssey to him—and he listened intensely. I was amazed at how intelligent and sympathetic he was, for his young age, so I treated him as an adult and we had a good chat. I gave him a few dollars, which he didn't want to take; I suggested that he take the money to his parents, who I was sure would put it to good use—and to tell his parents that he became friends with a tourist who was born in *Banes* and I merely paid him for his sightseeing services—which he did provide. Putting it in this perception, he agreed to take the money. I said goodbye to my new friend, who had the handshake of an adult: strong and meaningful.

Without delay, Pinto and I went straight to the Children's Park—which was a short block away. We made a left turn and then a quick right, and we were facing the steps that—to me—at the time were an endless task to walk up. The cement stairs led us to the entrance of the playground, which still boasted the same arched sign that read—*Parque Infantil*—now peeling and covered with rust. I cleared the stairs two steps at a time and stood at the top with my arms raised over my head "a la Rocky Balboa." I wanted to scream, "I'm King of the hill," but I suppressed my emotions—in order not to scare the women and children that were playing in the playground. Pinto, already thought I was crazy; but he confessed that he had never had so much fun with a tourist like he has had with me; besides, I was a special person, on a special mission, and that interested him. Pinto followed me into the play area and sat on a cement bench under a tree—far enough to give me private space, but near enough to come to my rescue if something nasty happened. My little friend, José, made a welcomed appearance and joined me on the rides. He was the perfect playmate; my little pal made me feel like a big kid. There were no grassy areas to roll around in—or have a picnic; the kids all played joyously in the dirt—even though they got it in their eyes, their hair, their clothing—they may even have eaten the dirt. Then again, it's what you're accustomed to. In my day, we had to play and keep reasonably clean at the same time; a dirty kid was unheard of. (What's a mother to do?) I kicked a lot of dirt in my day—even threw some.

The same swings and every contraption that went round "n" round were still here. One particular ride—I remembered the most—made me happy and nostalgic—almost, to the point of tears. It was the 'Boat Swing'—a boat shape swing suspended from extra long chains, for riding higher than was necessary. Melba would stand on one end of the boat, with me on the other end, and we'd pull back and forth, riding higher 'n' higher. This was our favorite ride. Melba was the tomboy in the family; but, don't get me wrong, she loves her men. Melba fought most of my battles; whenever she saw me running home from school, she knew that someone was out to get me. She always rescued and protected me. Even to this day, she plays the 'Mother Hen' role very well. Looking back, we had so much fun—those early years.

José and I climbed on the rusty 'Boat Swing'—to the squeaking tune of the grinding chains and me yelling, "Melba, eat your heart out." The chains squeaked so loud that my driver—fearing that José and I might get hurt or break the swing—made us get off. At one time, my whole body sat inside the small boat; now, I only managed to get one foot inside the vessel. The playground was much smaller than I perceived it to be. Although the park was rundown and everything was rusting and coming apart, I had a wonderful time playing; especially with my new friend who—somehow—magically—took me back in time. I said goodbye to José again and, this time, we hugged. "Will you come back and see me again?" he asked. With emotions running high, I replied, "Yes, José, I will be back. I don't know when, but I'll be back and I won't forget you."

I read off the first address where I wanted to go; it wasn't really an address, it was a section of town—*El Reparto La Gloria*. Once there, I'll ask the older residents if they knew of the Infante and Castellanos families. Nothing looked familiar—as we rode up and down dirt roads with potholes that could have easily damaged the car. *Walking is the best way to travel in these parts; riding a horse is the next best thing.* I searched for my house that had the only water well in the area— located in the backyard. I never found the house with the well; it was probably covered over by the grass and weeds that had overtaken the landscape. It was important for me to find the house where I was born in and—just as important— being in this space: in my old neighborhood. Most of the homes looked basically alike—made of wood, with bars on the windows, and painted in pastel colors. Our house was a light gray color and was surrounded by palms and flowers. The streets were wide and the houses were far apart from each other, with large fenced yards—usually with a pig or a goat tied to a post.

Back then no one needed an alarm clock; everyone had chickens and roosters that sang every morning—at the same time—sounding like a grand chorus. The day would start early with a bright sky and end with a spectacular sunset or a thunderous rainfall that usually ended in a very short time—giving way to a magnificent, blue velvet sky filled with stars so bright you could almost touch them. All of this is still true, except that the streets are now narrower and the houses and yards are much smaller and closer together. The whole neighborhood had been condensed into a smaller scale than what my mind had originally created. It felt both good to be here—and strange at the same time.

Silhouetted at the top of a small hill, stood a man in the middle of the road—wearing a white tee-shirt and black pants, which reminded me of my father. That hill was where I had played baseball with Papá. He would pitch to me and, of course, I would miss the ball—most of the time. I stood on the downside of the hill, so I often had to run all the way to the bottom—chasing the rolling ball. That was how I got my exercise and Papá didn't have to pitch so much. A baseball player I wasn't going to be.

We stopped the car to let two young men cross the road; they were carrying a freshly-killed pig for a birthday celebration. I took a picture and earned an invitation. The man on the hill seemed to be waiting for me. Something inside told me that he was the person to ask about my family. He seemed old enough and should remember, so I asked him of the families and he replied, "The Infante family moved from these parts many years ago, between 1945 and 1948. They lived in the gray house down the hill, that's half torn down. They went to the United States and we never heard from them again. Nice family, very reputable." No wonder I couldn't find the house, it was being demolish. "My name is Martinez, and as far as the Castellanos family, there is a woman by that name who lives in the house next to where you parked your car."

"Hello, is anyone home?" A frail, thin, old woman—about five feet tall—answered the door—her blue eyes inquisitively searching mine. I explained who I was and the purpose for my visit. She got very excited; she knew the family name and told me, as she hugged me, that she was my first cousin on my mother's side. She fired a million questions at me, while giving me a tour of the house, starting with the backyard, where she had a huge hog lounging in its own muddy corral; he was being fattened to become the guest of honor at the Christmas dinner, but the hog didn't know it. In another gated corral, there was another thin, but perky and extremely noisy, hog. This pig was going to meet its maker the following year. We entered the house by the dirt floor kitchen and she instantly started to prepare coffee—the old fashion way. Later, we passed by a tiny bedroom that led to the front door and the small, but nicely decorated, parlor with two chairs and a couch—with embroidered doilies placed neatly upon the backs and arms of the antique furniture. Knick-knacks and family pictures rested on the windowsills and—on the table, a bouquet of plastic flowers. A humongous photo of Jesus Christ hung on the wall—also enshrined with plastic flowers, joined with the usual statues of Saints. She was obviously a very religious woman. An old, but working, refrigerator and a television set completed the portrait of this humble home. Looking around the room, my thoughts were many: "This could have been me, I thought, living in this humble home made of unpainted cement blocks

and dirt floors, and living with muddy animals and smelling rancid food." I looked up towards the heavens and make the sign of the cross—thanking my father for having the sense and courage to move on to better pastures.

Alicia served the coffee and we sat for awhile—talking about Cuba and the government and, most of all, the families. The time we spent together was heart warming. She insisted we visit my second cousins before leaving. Everyone was taking the afternoon *siesta* when we arrived at the house half a block away; but Alicia's strong voice announced my visit and woke everyone from their slumber. More coffee was immediately served. They were so hospitable with what little they had to offer that I felt like I was taking something precious away from them. They offered me their homes for my next visit and promised to kill a hog in my honor. "That's some honor," I thought—rolling my eyes back into my head. "I'd rather the pig stay alive, thank you." After a heavy hugging session, I said goodbye—until the next time we meet again—but not until I had the pleasure of meeting my other first cousin—who—I was informed by the musicians, when I got back to the hotel—was a very colorful and renown character in these parts. I wasn't aware that I was related to such a grand celebrity. It seems that my cousin was the town's drunk. (No relation to the homeless clown in the park.) *Papo* was a classier bum; he got drunk, danced, sang loudly, and eventually—ended up in a fight. *Papo*, unfortunately, is not as handsome as the rest of the family; he looks like an aging 'Dopey'—one of the seven dwarfs of "Snow White." He is also the recipient of large, protruding, bigger-than-Chiclets teeth—always smiling and rubbing his head. My musician friends enjoyed being with *Papo*—and his antics—whenever they play in *Banes*, but *Papo* sometimes becomes so obnoxious that—sadly—he ends up with a black eye and has to be put to sleep. Most of the time he just passes out and someone deposits his limp, bruised body on the front door of his house.

The house where I was born was situated on the other side of town—not far from the center square and two blocks from the main street. *El Callejon de la Lechusa* or, as we say in English, "Owl Alley," was the house in which a *flamboyán* tree grew from the center of the kitchen and straight out through the roof. *Practical homemakers might inquire: "When it rains, wouldn't it flood the kitchen?"* Good question—but no, it didn't flood the kitchen. My father sealed the full-grown tree to the roof and ceiling with cement and the epoxy products that were available back then; so, the water that entered the house only dripped down the side of the tree—wetting its roots and providing sufficient water for it to survive. The remaining water would run off under the house and into the street. The *flamboyán* tree was too magnificent to cut down.

Cruising slowly down "Owl Alley," I searched for the address, but couldn't find the house. Pinto backed up a couple of times—to closely inspect the numbers, which didn't make sense, some numbers were missing and so were the houses—still, no house. Finally, we stopped and asked an elderly couple, sitting on the porch of a newly constructed home, "Do you, by any chance, know the Infante family that lived here?" Pinto asked. "The name sounds familiar. I think they lived in the house next door," the old man said, as he curiously checked me out. Hearing the commotion—which was put into play because of my overwhelming desire to find the house where my life began—the neighbors began to exit from their homes. Two elderly ladies in their late seventies, with jet black (obviously tinted) hair, emerged from another newly-prefabricated house: "We knew the family very well. We were friends and neighbors for many years, until they moved to America." When I was growing up, I often heard my family speak fondly of the eccentric dark hair duo. "The government gave us this property last year and we built this new house, but we ran out of money and couldn't finish the second floor. Your house had been vacant and in ruins for many years, so the government finally tore it down, including the celebrated flamboyán tree. Now it's just an empty lot, awaiting construction of a new home. It looked just like that old gray house next door, where my sister and I lived until a year ago; my cousins have it now." Their house was gray in color and made of wood. I examined it carefully, picturing in my mind what my home must have looked like. "Not so bad for it's time," I thought. "I'm sure in its hey-day, it must have been beautiful; so, I didn't feel so bad. Suddenly, my heart started to sink to the pit of my stomach, as my eyes filled with tears. I wanted to cry—I did cry. If only I hadn't procrastinated and visited here last year, I would have found my house—still standing. I felt like I had lost the 'start' of me. I was no longer able to place a plaque on the side of the house that would read, "JOEY INFANTE WAS BORN HERE." It was a stupid thought and I knew it was of no great importance; besides, the plaque would never have been placed anyway. Now, I can only say: "I was born in *Banes*—NO ADDRESS.

"My nick name is *Papi*, I am María's youngest son—searching for my roots, friends, and family." The glassy-eye sisters hugged me and tried to console me—patting my face gently; others came to listen to my stories down memory lane. They had many questions to ask, as well as stories to tell about my parents, my sisters, my brother—and how I was the terror of the neighborhood—but still loved by everyone: the prize child of *Banes*.

An impromptu block party was in effect—people came to meet me and share many new stories—new to my ears. Even though I regretted not seeing my house—which was my umbilical cord to *Banes*—I was content just being here—in the place and space of my true awakening—among such warm people. "This is your home.....look around you.....Cuba is your home.....the house merely gave you shelter." Surprisingly enough those words gave me great comfort; they were poetically put by a stranger, who left the circle—as mysteriously as he entered.

A sad-eye lady made her way through the crowd and threw her arms around me. "I too knew your family very well. Your sister, Cachita, and I were very good friends. After she married, she moved to the house next to the Children's Park." I gave her a bear hug and urged her to please help me find Cachita's house. I told her that Pinto and I had been driving up and down the streets, searching for the house, but never found it. My family stayed in Cachita's house for a year, before leaving for the United States; this house also held many memories for me. I remember it as a two-story house, with spacious rooms painted in green and divided by arches. The house was decorated with expensive antique furniture, brought over from Europe. Cachita had married well and had everything she wanted; but with all the material possessions, she was never really happy. She dedicated her life to raising her two children and, later, made it to America—where she became a liberated woman.

Pinto was leaning against the car, shaking his head in awe; he couldn't get over the intense reunion and he was proud to have been a part of it. I certainly couldn't have done this without his help.

We parted from the group and drove off in search of Cachita's house.

We passed the center of town—once again—and the sad-eye woman pointed out a vacant corner store, where she and her husband were owners of the *Fin de Ciglo* (End of The Century) store. I loved that store; during Christmas, the toys were all displayed in the window— illuminated with colored lights. Now, she owns nothing—everything was taken away by the new regime, leaving her with premature wrinkles on her face—from hard times.

In sight—once again—was the entrance to the children's playground. "There!" She pointed. "On the right was your sister's house." I got out of the car and a young woman, carrying a baby, came out to the porch. "Can I help you?" she asked. "No," I answered—as I walked towards her. "I was born here, in *Banes*, and I am now visiting for the first time since 1948. My sister once owned this house and I wanted to bring home a picture of what it looks like now. Is it OK, if I take a picture?" She nodded "yes" and gave me permission to take all the pictures I wanted. "Would you like to come inside the house?" "No, thank you, you're very kind, but that won't be necessary. I respect the privacy of your home." She waved and took the baby back inside the house.

I took all the photos I wanted and videotaped the unpainted, somber house and drove off to take Daisy home. The neighbors were still milling about outside—chatting about my unexpected visit, while waiting for our return. I stayed a while longer and then made my departure—from a perfect day that will remain in my memory—for a lifetime. My stay here in *Banes* had been—and will be—unforgettable; what I had set out to do has been accomplished. I will always remember my friends from the past and the new acquaintances who have helped make my trip a grand success.

We had a quiet trip back to the hotel and Pinto was sensitive enough—and gave me space so that I could reflect on this incredible walk through time. A brilliant sunset encompassed the sky with colors of orange and red, then changing to coral, then blending into blazing gold—a Technicolor finish to both a perfect and imperfect day. *Imperfect?* Yes, because I didn't find what I expected; and what I expected was either in ruins or ready to become one.

Time stood still in *Banes*—and by doing so, gave me the opportunity to trace my life before the day I left. It showed me my humble beginnings—that helped mold me into the person that I am today. Experiencing this roller coaster ride made me wonder what my life would have been like, if I had stayed; and I appreciate more what I have today. Few changes were made from 1941 to 1948, but after 1959 it was already too late. Fidel Castro took charge of the Island—destroying the morale of the people—their laughter—the shine in their eyes—their essence for living—and their desire to remain in the Garden of Eden. Fortunately, he couldn't destroy what is naturally beautiful; the country itself; the landscape; the flowers; the innocence. The young people (and the envious people) envisioned Cuba as a better place to live; later, to discover a life of begging for dollars in the streets and prostituting themselves, their wives, their sisters, and even their daughters—in order to survive. *Banes* and the entire island of Cuba has been paralyzed in time—deteriorating slowly from years of incarceration. In the last few years, the Cuban government has made extensive repairs throughout the island—for the benefit and enjoyment of the tourists, who are sadly experiencing a lie—a magnificent façade—showing them a great time and stripping them of their dollars. I admit that I had a wonderful time in Cuba and I will repeat my visit.....many more times; but I will never lose perspective of the present reality. I traveled like a native and did what I had to do—but with a broken heart for a broken people.

The wonderful memories of my childhood are still there; only today, they are in shambles and not pretty to look at. Remember Thomas Mann, who said, "You can't go home again." Yes, home is no longer what I relished and remembered. I thank GOD for enlightening my father, in his quest for a better place to live and raise his children. He knew it was time to go and search for another place to call home; he felt the change and corruption in the government; he felt the threatening presence of Fidel Castro—slowly closing in. I also want to thank GOD for his guidance in helping me find my roots and the grand, once-in-a-lifetime, opportunity to relive the first six years of my life—even if it was just for one day. I have emerged a better man—proud of my heritage and the humble beginnings that played an important role in molding me.....I am a Cuban.

EL FIN

Poem

Cuba

*Cuba—my long lost Island—I have finally touched you—after fifty-
five years of yearning to be cradled in your fertile red earth.
How I dreamt to dress in your leaves of multiple greens.
How I longed to inhale the rich scent of the flowers and fruits that
adorn your majestic trees.
I bathe in the unsurpassed essence of your tobacco fields—on a
wet, rainy day.
The mist of musk that perfumes the banks of your rivers, where the
fluttering dragonflies rest, brings me peace—while the serenade of
tiny frogs, nestled on the lily pads, strum out a lullaby, lulling me to
sleep.
I have walked your sunken valleys and climbed your rolling hills.
With the birds, I fly in the open sky and dive into deep lagoons.
I danced to the rhythm of life—to love—to death—and to the
breath that you gave to me.
It is not over between you and me—dear country—again, you shall
see me depart—but not for long.
Look for me in the shadows—OH, CUBA—for that is where—
deeply hidden—you will find my heart.*

By Joey Infante

Joey's Family Tree

Mother............María Luz Castellanos
Father..............Sandalio Infante

Children
Rodolfo ....Daughter.....Daisy
Son..........Rudy
Cachita.............Daughter.....Amelixis (a.k.a. Tania)
Son..........José Manuel
Misael...............Daughter.....Marilyn
Son...........Robert
Melba...............Daughter.....Lesley
Son...........George
José Carlos, (a.k.a. Joey).....Bachelor at Large
Children?.......all the above & below

Grand Nieces.................Natalie, Aria
Grand Nephews............Elijah, George II
Grand, Grand Nephew....Jonathan

**Names left out of this list have not participated in my life.

María Luz Castellanos and Sandalio Infante in Cuba

Family

From left to right:
Cachita, Mamá, Misael, Papá, Rodolfo

Joey as an infant in Cuba

Sister Melba, Age 4

y, Age 6

Sister Cachita

Joey and Mom, María

Joey

Joey and Musical
Director, James M. McDonald

Cuba

Joey's Paintings

Joey Infante was born in Banes, a small town in the Province of Oriente, Cuba, and grew up in Bridgeport, Connecticut. His natural talents led his teachers to recommend that he pursue a career in the arts. After being accepted to the "Famous Artists School" in Westport, Connecticut, Joey studied with the renowned American artist, Norman Rockwell, who encouraged Joey to paint what he felt. Joey also pursued the fields of voice and dance in preparation for a life in the theater. While appearing in "Oklahoma" at the Westport Country Playhouse, he was discovered by Richard Rodgers, which led to roles in the Broadway productions of "West Side Story," "Brigadoon," and many Off-Broadway productions (both in the English and Spanish languages). In New York City, Joey attended the "Stella Adler School of Drama." The art of make-up, costume and stage design, choreography and music helped prepare Joey for his varied forms of artistic expression. Joey's other credits include working with renowned Cuban composers, Julio Gutierrez (considered the Gershwin of Latin America) and Bobby Collazo. Joey worked with Gutierrez for five years, including a tour of the major hotels in Puerto Rico, Miami, and South America. As a teenager, Joey also appeared on Dick Clark's American Bandstand. Joey's artwork has been exhibited in the galleries of The West Side Arts Coalition, The Cork Gallery of Lincoln Center, The National Arts Club, The Museum of the City of New York, Taller Boricua, New York City's Libraries, and in private exhibitions. In June of 2003, Joey made his European debut with a solo show in Gordes, France, where he exhibited fifty new works based on his extensive travel throughout his homeland of Cuba. Joey is an active member of The West Side Arts Coalition.